100  FACTS

SOUTHAMPTON

100 FACTS

SOUTHAMPTON

Steve Horton

Bedford, England

First published in Great Britain in 2021
by Wymer Publishing
www.wymerpublishing.co.uk
Wymer Publishing is a trading name of Wymer (UK) Ltd

First edition. Copyright © 2021 Steve Horton / Wymer Publishing.

ISBN 978-1-912782-79-6

Edited by Jerry Bloom.

The Author hereby asserts his rights to be identified
as the author of this work in accordance with sections
77 to 78 of the Copyright, Designs & Patents Act 1988.

All rights reserved. No part of this publication may be
reproduced or transmitted in any form or by any means,
electronic or mechanical, including photocopying, or any
information storage and retrieval system, without written
permission from the publisher.

This publication is sold subject to the condition that it shall not,
by way of trade or otherwise, be lent, re-sold, hired out or
otherwise circulated without the publishers prior consent in any
form of binding or cover other than that in which it is published
and without a similar condition including this condition
being imposed on the subsequent purchaser.

Typeset and Design by Andy Bishop / 1016 Sarpsborg
Printed by CMP, Poole, Dorset

A catalogue record for this book is available from the British Library.

Sketches © Becky Welton-Fodder & Amy McIsaac.

FACT 1

1885
ST MARY'S
YOUNG MEN'S ASSOCIATION

The club that went on to become Southampton FC was formed in 1885 by members of the Young Men's Association (YMA) of St Mary's Church.

The YMA believed that strong limbs and a supple frame were important traits needed to ensure the appropriate moral character. They already had a gymnasium and competed in athletics and cricket. In November 1885 members met at school rooms in Grove Street and decided to form a football club, with the Reverend Arthur Baron Sole as its first president.

A friendly was arranged for 21st November with Freemantle, the leading club in the area. On the back field of the County Ground, St Mary's wore white shirts with red diagonal sashes, white shorts and black socks. They won 5-1, with Ned Bromley hitting a hat trick and Albert Fry scoring the other two goals. The *Southampton Times* reported that YMA "have among their members the materials with which to form a fairly strong club."

For the first two seasons of their existence St Mary's only played friendlies, with Southampton Common being used for 'home' games.

FACT 2

1887
THE ANTELOPE GROUND

In 1887 St Mary's YMA began playing some of their home fixtures at the Antelope Ground. This was part of their drive to be taken seriously by the game's governing bodies.

For two years the club played most of their home games at Southampton Common, which was not enclosed and even had a footpath running across the pitch. The formation of the Hampshire FA and inauguration of a county cup competition in 1887 meant they needed to look for a new venue to host competitive games where a charge could be made for admission.

The Antelope Ground, off St Mary's Road, was shared by a rugby club named Pirates and a football team, Woolston Works. The first St Mary's game there was on 17th December 1887 against Petersfield, who were thrashed 10-0 in the second round of the Hampshire Junior Cup.

For the next eighteen months the club played occasional fixtures at the Antelope Ground. Then in the summer of 1889 Woolson Works folded, allowing St Mary's the opportunity to become joint tenants with another rugby club, Trojans.

The Antelope Ground was neatly enclosed with one stand and grass banking on the other three sides. Players changed at the All England Eleven inn. Its limitations were exposed however at an FA Cup tie with Sheffield Wednesday in 1896 and the club opted to move again.

FACT 3
1888
HAMPSHIRE
JUNIOR CUP WINNERS

St Mary's YMA claimed their first trophy in 1888. They won the inaugural Hampshire Junior Cup, beating Southampton Harriers in the final after a replay.

After a 1-0 win at Totton in the first round, St Mary's were then drawn at home to Petersfield. The opposition had only ten men available and paid a price, St Mary's running out 10-0 winners at the Antelope Ground.

In the quarter final St Mary's were drawn at home to Lymington. The Antelope Ground was unavailable so the fixture was played at Redbridge, where St Mary's won 4-0.

Bournemouth Arabs were the opposition in the semi-final at the County Ground. St Mary's fell behind but came back to win 2-1, Ned Bromley scoring a late winner.

The County Ground also hosted the final, played between St Mary's and Southampton Harriers on 10th March. Harriers took a two-goal lead but St Marys fought back to draw 2-2, Bromley's equaliser coming three minutes from time.

Two weeks later the sides met again at the same venue. St Mary's won 2-1 thanks to goals from MacDonald and Warn. The *Southampton Times* reported that, "Though the Harriers played a great game, the St. Mary's played better football."

FACT 4

1894
SOUTHAMPTON ST MARY'S
JOIN THE SOUTHERN LEAGUE

In 1894 St Mary's YMA changed their name to Southampton St Mary's and were founder members of the Southern League.

The Southern League was formed to provide regular competitive matches for the best clubs in southern England that were not part of the Football League. Initially St Mary's were not invited to join the nine-club league, despite the majority of their players being professionals.

The club were thrown a lifeline when the league announced that a second division would be formed. However, the withdrawal of the 2nd Scots Guards from the top division led to Southampton St Mary's, as they had rebranded themselves, being invited to compete there anyway.

Saints first Southern League fixture was against Chatham on 6th October 1894 at the Antelope Ground. They won 3-1 in a game that saw a Chatham player sent off for complaining to the referee that Saints' second goal had been handball.

At the beginning of the season a correspondent in the *Southampton Times* predicted that Saints would finish no lower than third. The article also stated that only Millwall and Luton were stronger. It proved to be right, as Saints finished third, eight points behind champions Millwall who pipped Luton on goal average.

FACT 5

1896
THE COUNTY GROUND

Southampton St Mary's had to look for a new home in 1896 after the closure of the Antelope Ground. This led to them agreeing a deal to play games at the home of Hampshire Cricket Club.

Saints had the option to purchase the Antelope Ground but the committee couldn't agree a price with the freehold owners. The club also had to consider that further costs would be incurred by improvements needed to deal with the increasing number of spectators attending matches.

Thankfully Saints' president Henry Bencraft was also secretary of the cricket club. He was able to secure use of their ground for matches at a rental of £200 a per year. The Antelope Ground was then sold for housing development.

Saints were no strangers to the County Ground. They had hosted exhibition games there and also played in cup competitions. Their opening Southern League game was against Chatham on 19th September. On a sunny day in front of 4,000 spectators, John Farrell scored the opening goal in a 4-1 victory.

The County Ground remained Saints' home for two years before they were on the move again, this time to somewhere they would stay for over a century.

FACT 6
1897 SOUTHERN LEAGUE CHAMPIONS

In their first season at the cricket ground, and last as Southampton St Mary's, the club had great success. They won the Southern League title without losing a game and also reached the second round of the FA Cup.

Saints won their first nine games of the season. Five of these were at home, in which they scored 31 times. After Christmas their league form slowed a little. This was partly due to the demands of the FA Cup, in which Saints beat Cowes, Reading and Swindon in the qualifying rounds.

After disposing of Heanor Town in the first round, Saints were given a plum draw at home to Newton Heath (later Manchester United). 8,000 fans witnessed a 1-1 draw at the County Ground but they went on to lose the replay 3-1.

Back in the Southern League, Saints won 2-1 in their penultimate game at Wolverton on 14th April to secure the title. A crowd of 15,000 met the team on their return to Southampton Docks station, from where they paraded to Kingsland Square.

In the last match of the season, Saints drew 1-1 at home to Millwall to complete the twenty-game season unbeaten. During the close season the club became a limited company and the Board decided on a name change to Southampton FC.

FACT 7
1898
A CONTROVERSIAL
FA CUP SEMI FINAL

Southampton retained the Southern League championship in 1897-98. However, there was huge disappointment in the FA Cup as they were knocked out of the semi-final in controversial circumstances.

Saints finished in first place, four points ahead of Bristol City, who they beat in the FA Cup 3rd qualifying round. Further wins over Swindon and Eastville Rovers took them into the competition proper.

In the first round Saints beat Second Division Leicester Fosse 2-1 at the County Ground, becoming the first Southern League club to eliminate Football League opponents from the competition. They repeated this in the second round with a 1-0 home win over Newcastle.

In the quarter final Saints stunned First Division Bolton, winning a replay 4-0 at the County Ground after a 0-0 draw in Lancashire. Saints were paired with First Division opponents again in the semi-final. Despite centre forward John Farrell playing with an injury, they forced a 1-1 draw with Nottingham Forest.

In the replay at Crystal Palace the score was 0-0 with ten minutes left when the referee stopped the game due to a blizzard. When play resumed the snow was even worse and Saints' keeper George Clawley was unsighted for both of Forest's goals. Despite furious protests to the FA, the result stood, denying Saints a place in the final.

FACT 8

1898
THE DELL

Southampton finally had a ground to call their own home in 1898. They moved to a purpose-built venue at The Dell, where they would remain for 103 years.

The County Ground was only ever meant to be a short-term solution for Saints. They even considered a merger with Freemantle and a move to their ground in Shirley, but this soon fell through.

In 1897 shareholders at an extraordinary general meeting heard that a site had been identified for a new ground. It was a narrow valley with natural banking that would be ideal for spectators. A small steam had run through it but this had been culverted by its present owners as part of a railway development that was no longer taking place.

Director George Thomas bought the site, levelled it off for the pitch and built two covered stands. Behind one goal was banking with accommodation for 15,000 standing spectators in a total capacity of 24,000. Thomas spent about £9,000 and agreed a £250 per year lease with the club.

The first game at The Dell was on 3rd September. It was a baking hot day on which 6,524 spectators saw Watty Keay score the opening goal there as Saints beat Brighton United 4-1.

FACT 9
1899
SAINTS' FIRST SENDING OFF

On 7th January 1899 Arthur Chadwick became the first Southampton player to be sent off. He received his marching orders in a 2-1 Southern League defeat at Sheppey United.

Chadwick was a powerful defender that had signed from Burton Swifts in 1897. He started out at right half but was soon switched to the centre, where he was a great success.

The game at Sheppey was 1-1 at half time. Early in the second half Chadwick upended one of the home players, but no action was taken. A few minutes later. Sheppey went ahead in controversial circumstances by rushing the Saints keeper over the line whilst he had the ball.

Although Sheppey's goal was within the rules, Saints were incensed and refused to apologise for surrounding the referee. According to the *Athletic News*, they "lost their leads, so much so that Chawick, after repeated cautions, got his marching orders." The game finished 2-1, Saints first defeat of the season.

The *Weekly Dispatch* reported that Chadwick's sending off was for "foul play and impudence." The game's governing bodies didn't hold it against him and the following season he was twice capped by England. He left Saints in 1901, joining Portsmouth.

FACT 10
1899
3rd STRAIGHT TITLE WON IN DRAMATIC FASHION

In their first season at The Dell, Southampton won the Southern League for the third successive season. They won the title on the final day of the season, beating Bristol City in a winner takes all game at their St John's Lane ground.

Going into the last game, Saints were level on points with Bristol City but with a superior goal average. It meant that a win or draw would be enough for Saints to be champions.

400 Saints fans travelled to Bristol, where the home side had been undefeated all season. In the first half an injury to Saints keeper Jack Robinson limited his ability and at halftime they trailed 2-0.

Within fifteen minutes of the restart Saints had levelled the scores thanks to goals from Arthur Chadwick and Jock Robertson. With the Saints keeper needing protection, the forwards continued to take the game to City. Harry Wood set up Robertson for the third goal before heading in the fourth from a corner.

City pulled a late goal back but Saints held on for a 4-3 victory to secure a third straight title. When the Saints team arrived back in Southampton later that evening, they were met by cheering crowds. There was then a victory parade accompanied by the town band.

FACT 11
1899
FIRST
SOUTH COAST DERBY

The very first meeting between Southampton and their greatest rivals Portsmouth took place on 6th September 1899. In a friendly at Fratton Park, Saints were beaten 2-0.

Portsmouth had only been formed in 1898 and were accepted into the Southern League for the 1899-1900 season. This game was the first to be played at their new ground, Fratton Park.

In front of a crowd of 5,000 the game was kicked off by the Mayor of Portsmouth. Saints fell behind after ten minutes when Cunliffe scored with what the *Portsmouth Evening News* described as a "clinking shot." Soon after Alf Millward thought he had equalised but his effort was ruled out for offside.

Early in the second half Saints dominated the play but were repeatedly denied by the home keeper. Frustration then grew when Millward was ruled to be offside when in a great scoring position and Arthur Chadwick was spoken to by the referee for repeated fouling.

Clarke doubled Portsmouth's lead and there was no way back for Saints. Their best chance was from a free kick that went wide and after the game one unnamed Saints player was reported to have told the home side "You have got together a very fine lot."

FACT 12
1900
FIRST SOUTHERN LEAGUE FA CUP FINALISTS

In 1899-1900 Southampton became the first team from the Southern League to reach the FA Cup final. However, it ended in disappointment when they were well beaten 4-0 by First Division Bury.

In the first three rounds Saints shocked topflight Everton, Newcastle and West Bromwich Albion at The Dell. They were drawn against fellow Southern League members Millwall in the semi-final. After a 0-0 draw at Crystal Palace, they won 3-0 in a replay at Reading.

The final at Crystal Palace was played on a baking hot day. Most of the neutrals in the 68,945 crowd were backing Saints, the first southern team since Old Etonians in 1883 to reach the final.

Bury started off the better side and went ahead after nine minutes. After a quarter of an hour Jack Robinson made a good save from Jack Plant but Willie Wood scored the rebound. Saints looked a beaten team with few attacking ideas and midway through the half Bury scored a third.

In the second half Robinson's fine goalkeeping prevented an embarrassing score line. He could do nothing however to prevent Plant's fierce shot going into the net ten minutes from time.

It had been hugely disappointing for Saints, whose performance was described by the *Athletic News* as "a weak, wavering, pitiable and lamentable show."

FACT 13
1901
FOURTH TITLE
IN FIVE SEASONS

Southampton made up for the disappointing defeat in the FA Cup final by winning the Southern League in 1900-01.

Several changes were made to the playing staff, including the addition of three players from First Division Everton: Bertram Sharp, George Molyneux and Wilf Toman. Former England international forward Edgar Chadwick was signed from Burnley, with Fred Harrison and Berty Lee being recruited from local sides.

It was their form at The Dell which was key to Saints' title success. They won thirteen and drew one of their fourteen home games. Chadwick proved to be a key signing, as he finished the club's top scorer with fourteen goals.

Saints took a huge step towards the title at home to Portsmouth on 6th April. A win for the visitors would see them close the gap to just one point, but Alf Milward scored twice in a 2-0 victory for Saints.

Two days after beating Portsmouth, Saints secured the title with a game to spare. On a bright and sunny day at The Dell, 6,000 spectators watched an entertaining 0-0 draw against Reading. This confirmed Saints as champions for the fourth time in the past five seasons.

FACT 14
1901 EUROPEAN TOUR

At the end of the 1900-01 season Southampton set off for their first foreign tour. They played seven games and won all of them, scoring fifty goals and conceding just three.

The Saints party sailed from Harwich on 20th April for an overnight crossing to Hook of Holland. Their first match was against Dutch champions HVV Den Haag, who were beaten 6-2.

The next destination was Prague, now capital of the Czech Republic but then part of the Austro-Hungarian Empire, where the remaining six fixtures of the tour would be played. Saints beat Slavia Prague 3-1 and stayed in the city to beat a combined Prague/Vienna select side 6-1.

In Vienna, Saints beat Vienna Cricket 7-0 and a city select side 6-1. The last stop of the tour was Budapest, where the Hungarian champions Budapest Torna were hammered 8-0. In the final game of the tour Saints thrashed a team of players selected from various Hungarian clubs 13-0. A Reuters telegram reported that "the British team kept the Hungarians entirely on the defensive."

On 3rd May the tour party arrived back in Southampton. The players told reporters they had the most enjoyable time and praised the hospitality in each city they visited.

FACT 15
1901
ALBERT BROWN'S
SEVEN GOALS IN A GAME

Southampton's 11-0 thrashing of Northampton on 28th December 1901 is a joint club record victory. Albert Brown scored seven of the team's goals, more than any other Saints player has got in a single game.

On a quagmire of a pitch, Brown scored the opening goal in less than a minute. He kicked off by playing the ball out to the wing, ran towards the box and received the return pass to score.

Saints were then under a brief period of pressure before Brown made it 2-0 from an Archie Turner cross. The crowd were still cheering when Turner crossed for Brown again, who headed it past the keeper. He had completed his hat trick with less than ten minutes gone.

Turner scored Saints' fourth goal, Samuel Meston the fifth and Brown the sixth. Frederick Harrison's goal meant it was 7-0 at half time. After the break Saints remained dominant and Meston scored the eighth. Brown then scored with an unstoppable shot, header and solo run to bring his own total to seven and complete an 11-0 rout.

This and the 11-0 win over Watford in December 1902 remain joint record victories. However, Brown had left by then. An injury at the start of that season meant he lost his place in the side and he was sold to Queens Park Rangers.

FACT 16
1902
BEATEN IN
FA CUP FINAL REPLAY

Southampton reached the FA Cup final again in 1902. Despite playing much better than in 1900, they were beaten by Sheffield United in a replay.

Saints beat holders Tottenham in a first round tie that required two replays. They then shocked Football League champions Liverpool, winning 4-1 at The Dell. In the third round they gained revenge on Bury, beating them 3-2 at Gigg Lane. The semi-final against Nottingham Forest was played at Tottenham's White Hart Lane, with Saints winning 3-1.

On 19th April, against Sheffield United at Crystal Palace, Saints went behind after 55 minutes, but two minutes from full time Harry Wood equalised. United appealed for offside and their keeper Willie 'Fattie' Foulke was so furious he tried to break into the referee's changing room after the game.

The replay a week later attracted a crowd of just 33,068 which was less than half which attended the first game. United scored after just two minutes but Saints remained calm and midway through the second half Albert Brown equalised. Saints looked more likely to score the winner but Foulke was outstanding in goal.

With eleven minutes to go Saints keeper Jack Robinson couldn't reach a cross by Alf Common and Billy Barnes scored the winning goal. It was seventy-four years before Saints reached another FA Cup final.

FACT 17
1903
SOUTHAMPTON RECLAIM TITLE FROM PORTSMOUTH

Southampton won the Southern League for the fifth time in 1902-03. In doing so they took the trophy back from Portsmouth, who had been champions in 1902.

Saints had finished third the previous campaign but showed their intent with a 6-0 win over Brentford at The Dell in the first game of the season. They then drew 1-1 at home to Portsmouth, but remained unbeaten until Boxing Day, a run of fifteen games.

During the season Saints enjoyed some big wins, including an 11-0 thrashing of Watford at The Dell. They finished with a huge goal average of 4.150, scoring 83 and conceding just twenty in thirty games. Only two games were lost, both of them against Tottenham.

The title was secured on 4th April when Saints won 2-1 at Luton and closest challengers Reading could only draw at home to Tottenham. This meant Saints had a lead of five points with just two games to go.

On 13th April, Saints entertained West Ham at The Dell in the last game of the season. As the players took the field the Town Band played *The Conquering Hero* whilst the crowd cheered. Saints then showed no signs of easing up and played magnificently in a 6-0 win.

FACT 18

1904
SAINTS WIN EXPANDED SOUTHERN LEAGUE

Southampton retained the Southern League title in 1903-04. The league's expansion to eighteen clubs had no effect on Saints, who won the title by a bigger margin than the previous season.

At the end of 1902-03 just one team was relegated from the Southern League's top division and two promoted. Plymouth Argyle were then being elected directly to the topflight bringing the total number of teams to eighteen.

Saints had a shaky start, winning two and drawing three of their first six games. However, after a 3-1 win over Millwall on 10th October, they didn't go two or more games without a win for the rest of the season.

The title never looked in doubt although Saints weren't as spectacular as the season before. This time around they scored 75 goals from 34 games — eight less than they managed from thirty in 1902-03.

Despite leading all the way, Saints couldn't actually wrap the title up until their last game due to Portsmouth having games in hand. On 9th April at The Dell, George Hedley's second half goal gave Saints a 1-0 win over Brentford to confirm a sixth title.

When all the other games were concluded, Saints finished seven points ahead of second placed Tottenham, with Portsmouth a point further behind in fourth.

FACT 19
1904
SOUTH AMERICA

In 1904 Southampton created history by becoming the first team from a different continent to tour South America. They played six games in total, winning all of them comfortably.

A large crowd gathered on 3rd June to wave the Saints players off as they sailed for Buenos Aires on the *Danube*. Their visit was eagerly anticipated in Argentina, which in 1891 had been the first country outside the British Isles to start a league.

All five of Saints' matches in Buenos Aires were played at the Sociedad Sportiva. The first was on 26th June when Alumni were beaten 3-0, then on 3rd July Britanicos were thrashed 10-0.

On 6th July Saints beat Belgrano 6-1, then hammered the national side 8-0. Their last game there on 10th July was the most testing one, in which Saints ground out a 5-3 victory over a composite Argentine League XI.

The Saints party then crossed the River Plate to Montevideo, the capital city of Uruguay. In a game played against a backdrop of revolutionary rioting in the city, Saints beat a Uruguay League XI 8-1 on 14th July.

On 12th August the players arrived back at Southampton. They were described as being "in the best of spirits" and praised the hospitality they had been offered.

FACT 20
1909
SOUTHAMPTON SHIRTS FOR SPANISH GIANTS

In 1909 a Spanish student bought fifty Southampton shirts when he was in the city. When he got home, they became the colours of two clubs who are amongst the most famous in Spain.

Juan Elorduy was sailing back to Bilbao from Southampton and liked the fact that the red and white striped shirts were the same colours of the flag of his home city. He decided to buy fifty of them before embarking for home.

The following year the city's club, Athletic Bilbao started wearing these shirts instead of their usual blue and white halves. Surplus shirts were sent to Atletico Madrid, who had been formed earlier that decade by students from the Basque region, where Bilbao is situated. They changed from blue and white halves to red and white stripes in 1911.

The two Spanish club's previous colours had been inspired by Blackburn. When the changes came, Athletic Bilbao switched to black shorts but Atletico Madrid continued to wear blue and both traditions continue today.

The clubs are two of the most successful in Spain after Real Madrid and Barcelona. Athletic Bilbao have won eight La Liga titles and never been relegated, while Atletico Madrid have enjoyed European success, winning the Europa League three times.

FACT 21
1920
THE FOOTBALL LEAGUE

Southampton became members of the Football League for the 1920-21 season. Along with most of the other Southern League clubs, they became founder members of the new Third Division.

The Third Division essentially consisted of the same clubs who made up the Southern League in 1919-20. The exceptions were Cardiff City who were elected to the Second Division and Grimsby Town, who were relegated from there.

Arthur Dominy scored Saints first Football League goal on 28th August in a 1-1 draw at Gillingham. Saints lost just one of their opening sixteen games and were top of the table going into the New Year.

A disappointing January and February, in which Saints won just two games from seven, saw them drop down to third. With only the champions being promoted, it was always going to be a struggle to overhaul Crystal Palace who had hit form at just the right time.

Saints lost just once in their last fourteen games, but seven of these were drawn including two against Palace. In the first of these at The Dell, Palace scored a last-minute equaliser. It meant Saints finished the season in second place, five points adrift of the London side.

FACT 22
1921
LONGEST UNBEATEN RUN

Southampton's longest run of games without defeat happened in the first half of the 1921-22 season. They were unbeaten in nineteen games over a four-month period.

Saints embarked on the run after a 2-0 defeat at Gillingham on 3rd September. In their next game Saints beat Luton 2-1 at home, the first of six successive wins.

The winning run came to an end with a 2-2 draw at Norwich on 8th October but the following week the same opposition were beaten 2-0 at The Dell. They then drew 1-1 at Watford before winning the return fixture 2-0.

Saints then won 1-0 at Reading but could only draw 0-0 with them at home. They then beat Charlton 6-0 at The Dell on 19th November. This was the start of another six-game winning streak, the last of these being an 8-0 thrashing of Northampton at home on Christmas Eve.

On Boxing Day Saints drew 2-2 at Queens Park Rangers and the following day the two sides drew 0-0 at The Dell. The run extended to nineteen games on New Year's Eve with a 0-0 draw at home to Brentford.

Saints were finally beaten on 14th January 1922 when they lost 2-0 at Brentford. They had won thirteen and drawn six of the games, scoring 41 goals and conceding eleven.

FACT 23
1922
THIRD DIVISION
SOUTH CHAMPIONS

Southampton were promoted in 1921-22 as champions of the Third Division South. In a thrilling finish to the season, they won their last three games to pip Plymouth Argyle, finishing above them on goal average.

The Football League was expanded again for this season with the creation of Third Divisions North and South, with only the top club in each earning promotion.

Saints lost just once in their first 22 games and were top of the table at New Year. However, two wins from six during January saw them fall below Plymouth who were the only other realistic challengers for promotion.

Saints had a solid defence that conceded just 21 goals, but they drew too many games and were unable to pull clear of Plymouth. On 15th April Saints lost 1-0 at Plymouth, meaning with seven games left they were five points adrift, although they did have two games in hand.

On the final day of the season Saints were at home to Newport County, needing a win coupled with a Plymouth defeat to go up. Saints stormed to a 5-0 victory and fans then waited anxiously for their rivals' score. When it was announced that Plymouth had lost 2-0 at Queens Park Rangers fans went wild with excitement as they celebrated promotion to the Second Division.

FACT 24
1923
A PERFECTLY EVEN SEASON

Southampton's first season in the Second Division was remarkably average. In addition to finishing mid table in eleventh place, they had the same number of wins, draws and losses, as well as the same number of goals for and against.

Saints started the season poorly, failing to score in any of their first five games and not winning until they a 2-1 victory at Blackpool in their seventh fixture. This was the start of a steady climb up the table which saw them well clear of the relegation places by the end of November.

Although Saints struggled at times in December and January, they tended to lose against the promotion chasing teams but picked up points from those who were struggling. In early March they even crept into the top half of the table for a brief period.

A 2-0 home win over Clapton Orient on 14th April was Saints' sixth game without defeat. It meant that with four games left they were closer in terms of points to the promotion places than the relegation ones.

Saints lost three of their last four games, meaning they finished the season with a record of fourteen wins, fourteen draws and fourteen defeats. Amazingly they also had an equal goal average, with forty for and forty against.

FACT 25
1928
A NEW WEST STAND

There was a major upgrade at The Dell in 1928 when a new West Stand was completed. The rebuilding work increased the ground capacity by more than 50% and also meant the club secretary needed to find somewhere else to live.

The original West Stand ran for just seventy yards because at the Archers Road corner was a house. Just one row of spectators could stand between its wall and the touchline. The house was occupied by the secretary while the wall was used for adverts.

Saints employed the famous Scottish engineer Archibald Leitch for the project. He designed a two-tier structure with 4,500 seats above a paddock with standing room for 8,500. The balcony had Leitch's familiar criss-cross steelwork.

At the same time, the East paddock was reprofiled, providing some additional standing room. This raised the ground capacity from 20,000 to 33,000.

The new stand was officially opened on 7th January 1928 by William Pickford, one of the founder members of the Hampshire FA who was known as 'the father of football' in the county.

Leitch himself was in attendance, along with the Mayor and local Member of Parliament. Marion Knight sang *Land of Hope and Glory* but the result did not match the occasion, as Saints lost 4-1 to Leeds.

FACT 26

1929
FIRE IN
THE EAST STAND

Southampton's East Stand was destroyed by fire in 1929. The blaze occurred after the last game of the season and it was a miracle that nobody was killed or injured.

On 4th May Saints beat Swansea 3-0 in front of a crowd of 6,510. It meant they finished fourth in the Second Division, their best position to date.

After all the players and officials had left the ground, a boy who was passing saw flames and immediately ran to the club offices to notify the secretary. By the time the fire brigade arrived, a strong wind had fanned the flames and the wooden structure was beyond salvage.

Investigations concluded that the fire had been started when a discarded cigarette fell through a crack and set light to litter. It was extremely good fortune that all players and fans had already left. Firemen were also able to prevent the flames spreading to an adjoining school.

The building of the West Stand had already stretched the club's finances and a further £10,000 had to be borrowed from the insurance company Norwich Union to fund a replacement. A new 2,500 seat stand was ready for the start of the next season, but it had come at the expense of team investment.

FACT 27
1934
NO AWAY WINS

Southampton failed to win any of their 21 away games in 1933-34. It was part of a club record 33 games without an away victory stretching across three seasons.

After five games Saints were third in the table thanks to victories in their three home games. However, their inability to win on the road meant they soon sank down the table. Thankfully they won fifteen home games, meaning they were never in any real danger of relegation.

Of the twenty-one away games, Saints drew six and lost fifteen. The defeats themselves were not heavy ones, with a 4-1 loss at Nottingham Forest the only time they were beaten by three goals or more. Despite such a dire away results record, they still conceded less away goals than fifteen other teams.

Saints away form didn't improve in 1934-35. They lost the first three away games of that campaign, scoring once and conceding eleven. The awful run finally came to an end on Christmas Day, when they won 1-0 at Swansea.

The victory over Swansea came in Saints' eleventh away game of the season. Adding the other ten games to the twenty-one from 1933-34, and the last two of 1932-33, it meant a sequence of thirty-three away games without a win.

FACT 28
1940
THE DELL IS BOMBED

During the Second World War Southampton were forced to play their home games elsewhere for a period due to The Dell being bombed in November 1940.

The Football League was suspended at the outbreak of war in September 1939. Teams were then allowed to play in localised competitions, with Saints being in the South Regional League.

The area around The Dell was bombed heavily due to it being just a mile from the docks. In November 1940 a bomb fell on the pitch at the Milton Road end. This left an eighteen-foot crater that also caused a culvert to break and flood the pitch.

Saints played the remainder of their league games that season away from home. However, when they were drawn at home to Brentford in the War Cup, they played the tie at Portsmouth's Fratton Park.

In March 1941 there was a further incident at The Dell when there was a fire caused by an explosion in munitions that were being stored there. Home games at the beginning of the 1941-42 season were played at Dew Lane, Eastleigh, before Saints were finally able to return to The Dell in October 1941.

FACT 29

1948
CHARLIE WAYMAN
SCORES FIVE

The only Southampton player to score five goals in a Football League game is Charlie Wayman. He did this on 23rd October 1948 when Saints beat Leicester City 6-0 at The Dell in a Second Division fixture.

Wayman's opening goal after twelve minutes was the 100th in the Football League for the striker who had signed from Newcastle a year earlier. He stroked the ball into the net from a pass by Wilf Grant. His second, on the half hour, was from close range and gave the keeper no chance.

Ted Bates made it 3-0 before half time then eleven minutes after the restart Wayman completed his hat trick with a headed goal from a corner. Four minutes later Eric Day set Wayman up for his fourth and Saints' fifth goal.

Wayman completed the scoring midway through the half. John Bradley's first effort was blocked by the keeper but only into the path of Wayman who headed the ball into an empty net.

During his time at Saints, Wayman scored 77 goals in 107 games. He left the club in 1950, signing for Preston as his wife wanted to return to the North.

FACT 30

1949
EIGHT POINT LEAD SURRENDERED

In 1948-49 Southampton surrendered an eight-point lead in the promotion race. After looking odds on to go up at the beginning of April, they won just one of their last seven games to finish third.

A run of twelve games unbeaten in the first three months of the year helped Saints build up a commanding lead at the top. With seven games left they were eight points clear of West Bromwich Albion in third, who did have two games in hand.

A 2-0 defeat at Bradford Park Avenue was followed by a 1-0 home loss to West Ham, who became the first visitors to win at The Dell that season. Over Easter, Saints won 1-0 at Grimsby on Good Friday, but then lost 1-0 at Bury on the Saturday. They then could only draw 0-0 at home with Grimsby on Easter Monday.

Despite this downturn in form, Saints could still secure promotion with a home victory over Albion on 23rd April. However, a 1-1 draw meant promotion was now out of their hands. The following week Saints lost their last game 1-0 at Chesterfield, leaving Albion needing just one win from two games to go up. They made no mistake, winning the first of these 3-0 at Leicester to end Saints' dreams of promotion.

FACT 31

1950
MISSING PROMOTION
BY 0.06 OF A GOAL

Promotion agony was suffered again in 1949-50. Despite being unbeaten for their last nine games, Southampton missed out by just 0.06 of a goal to Sheffield Wednesday

It was rarely in doubt that Tottenham would be promoted. They lost just one of their opening 25 games to create a big gap at the top. The second promotion place was much more open, with Saints battling against the two Sheffield clubs, United and Wednesday.

Saints were playing catch up after losing their first three games. They found their form in mid-September, when a 4-0 loss at Swansea was followed by just one defeat in the remaining fifteen games of 1949.

After losing 3-2 at home to Brentford on 18th March, Saints were sixth with nine games remaining. They beat United and Wednesday 1-0 in successive games in the middle of April but were still reliant on Wednesday dropping points. Saints then drew their next two games, away at Cardiff and Plymouth, seriously denting their chances.

In their final game, Saints needed to beat West Ham at The Dell and hope Wednesday lost at home to Spurs. Despite being 2-0 down at half time, Saints came back to win 3-2 but it wasn't enough. Wednesday drew 0-0 to go up, denying Saints by 0.06 of a goal.

FACT 32
1950
FIRST FLOODLIGHTS IN ENGLAND

Southampton were the first English football club to install permanent floodlights in 1950. The big switch on though was spoiled by dense fog that cut the game short.

The decision to install lights was made after Saints played under them on a tour of Brazil. Erected at a cost of £600, there were eight 1,800 watt lamps on each side of the ground that cost just six shillings an hour to power. Additional lights in the car park allowed local amateur players to train.

An exhibition match was arranged against Bournemouth on 31st October. There was such an interest generated that even the England manager, Walter Winterbottom, attended. However, despite the lights looking impressive, they weren't good enough to deal with the fog that descended on The Dell.

Due to several thousand spectators having turned out, the teams agreed to make the most of things and were able to play for an hour. They changed ends without a break after thirty minutes and although the crowd could follow the white ball, there were no goals.

The first official fixture under the lights was a year later when Saints reserves took on Tottenham in a Football Combination fixture.

FACT 33

1953
RELEGATED

1952-53, Ted Bates' last season as a club player, was a huge disappointment. A run of just one defeat in eight games at the end of the campaign was too late to save Saints from relegation to the Third Division.

On 20th December Saints stalwart Ted Bates made his last appearance for the club in a 2-1 defeat at home to West Ham. That loss left Saints in 21st place, one point from safety.

After a 5-0 defeat at Huddersfield on 21st March, Saints were five points from safety with eight games left. The first of these was against leaders Sheffield United at The Dell and Saints earned a creditable 4-4 draw.

The following week Saints won 1-0 at Barnsley, condemning the Yorkshire side to the drop. Their next three games were all at The Dell and ended in draws with Leeds and Birmingham and victory over Lincoln.

Next up was a crucial trip to Hull, who were four points ahead of Saints. It ended in a 1-0 defeat, meaning Saints now needed a miracle to stay up.

On 25th April, Eric Day scored a hat trick as Saints beat Blackburn 6-1 in their last home game of the season. However, it was too late to save Saints as their relegation was confirmed by results elsewhere. Bates didn't leave Saints though and was given a coaching role.

FACT 34
1957
TERRY PAINE'S DEBUT

Terry Paine made more appearances for Southampton than any other player. The first of these 816 games was against Aldershot on 23rd March 1957, when he scored in a 1-1 draw.

Paine was signed from Winchester City and in early March 1957 made his debut for both the 'A' and reserve sides, before being promoted to the first team for the trip to Aldershot, which fell on his 18th birthday. Playing on the left wing, he cut in to score Saints' goal and after the game manager Ted Bates told reporters that he was even better on the right.

The following season Paine made the number seven shirt, traditionally worn by the outside right, his own. He remained at the club until 1974, making 812 starts and four substitute appearances. Despite being a Second Division player, he was a member of England's 1966 World Cup winning squad, playing one group game against Mexico.

Paine left Saints in 1974, having scored 187 goals. He became player coach at Hereford, helping them to promotion to the second Division.

As of 2021 Paine now lives in South Africa and has a hospitality suite at St Mary's named after him. 785 of his Saints' appearances were for Ted Bates. This was a record under one manager until Ryan Giggs surpassed it playing with Sir Alex Ferguson as his boss at Manchester United.

FACT 35
1960
PROMOTED
AS CHAMPIONS

Southampton were promoted to the Second Division in 1959-60. Unlike in previous seasons they rarely looked like slipping up, finishing nine points clear of third place and scoring 106 goals.

Manager Ted Bates pulled off a masterstroke in the close season, selling striker Charlie Livesey to Chelsea in part exchange for midfielder Cliff Huxford. There was still £12,000 left which was spent on another midfielder, Dick Connor and forward George O'Brien.

The three new arrivals settled effortlessly into the side and Derek Reeves was moved to centre forward. Saints took the division by storm and were prolific at The Dell, scoring 68 goals in 23 home games.

Even when Saints only won two games out of eight in the spring it remained a case of when, not if, they would be promoted. Over Easter they had successive wins over Accrington and Reading at The Dell, meaning they needed just one point from their last three games to secure promotion.

Saints then secured their Second Division place without kicking a ball. On 20th April Coventry were beaten by Grimsby meaning Saints could not finish outside the top two. The title was wrapped up on the last day of the season as Saints beat Bradford City 2-0 at The Dell to finish two points ahead of Norwich and nine clear of third place Shrewsbury.

FACT 36
1960
DEREK REEVES
GOALSCORING RECORD

When Southampton were promoted in 1959-60, Derek Reeves finished as the club's top scorer with 45 goals in all competitions. This remains a club record and his total of 39 in the Third Division is also a record at that level.

Reeves signed for Saints in 1954 after finishing his National Service and soon established himself as a prolific centre forward. He was ready to pounce on any half chance and despite his lack of height, got his fair share of headed goals from the crosses of Terry Paine and John Sydenham.

For the past three seasons Reeves had been top scorer for Saints and he continued this form during the promotion season. He got 39 of Saints' 106 goals but his most memorable game was actually in the FA Cup. Saints stunned First Division Manchester City in the third round at Maine Road, winning 5-1 with Reeves scoring four of the goals.

In the Second Division Reeves struggled against tighter defences. He did remain at the club for two seasons but the arrival of George Kirby and emergence of Martin Chivers led to him being sold to Bournemouth in September 1962.

FACT 37
1961
RECORD CUP WIN

Southampton's biggest ever win in cup competition was on 7th January 1961. They thrashed Ipswich 7-1 at The Dell in the third round of the FA Cup.

George O'Brien started the rout in the seventh minute, seizing on a schoolboy defensive error to race clear and tuck the ball into the net.

Ipswich, who were pushing for promotion to the First Division, played attractive football but were repeatedly undone by Saints' direct style and ruthless punishment of errors. Saints were in devastating form and the only way Terry Paine could be stopped was by fouling him.

After half an hour it was 5-0, with four of the goals coming in a devastating seven-minute spell. Saints had scored a sixth by half time following a performance described by the *Sunday People* as "rip snorting."

The second half was far more even, with Saints unable to maintain the intensity of the first half and managing just one more goal. Ipswich continued to contribute to the game and forced some good saves from Ron Reynolds. Their one goal though was from a Saints player, when John Page deflected a shot into his own net.

The victory was even more impressive considering Ipswich finished as Second Division champions that season, with Saints in eighth.

FACT 38
1962 ANGLO-FRENCH FRIENDSHIP CUP

Southampton had their first taste of continental competition in 1961-62. They were one of the group of four English teams that were winners of the short lived Anglo-French Friendship Cup.

The cup pitted teams from England and France against each other. The trophy was awarded to the best league based on aggregate scores rather than an individual club. These would be determined by the results of four two-legged ties between clubs from the countries.

Saints' tie was against Bordeaux, who were also a Second Division club. The first game was at The Dell on 13th November 1961 and attracted a crowd of just 3,315. Saints won 2-1 thanks to a goal in the first half from David Chadwick and George O'Brien's free kick two minutes after the break.

The second game in France was not played for nearly six months. On 1st May 1962 Bordeaux won 2-0 to win their tie and leave the whole competition on a knife edge. England now led 2-1 with one game to play. That game took place two weeks later with Derby losing 2-1 in Beziers, but drawing 2-2 on aggregate.

Derby's tied tie meant that England were the series winners. This had been the second year of the Anglo-French Friendship Cup but it was never contested again.

FACT 39
1964
ONE HUNDRED GOALS

The only time Southampton have ever managed a century of goals in the top two divisions was in 1963-64. They scored exactly 100 but were still way off the promotion pace.

Saints started the season with a 6-1 hammering of Charlton at The Dell. They failed to win any of their next six games, but still had no trouble in attack, losing 5-4 to Preston in one game.

After losing 1-0 at Middlesbrough on 5th October 1963, Saints scored in their next seventeen games, a run that finally ended on 29th February 1964 when they lost 1-0 at home to Bury. High scoring victories in this period were 6-0 against Grimsby and 7-2 over Scunthorpe.

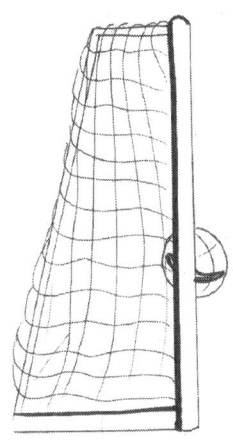

On 1st April Saints again scored four times despite being on the losing side when they went down 6-4 at Derby. Saints endured a couple of heavy defeats during the season, 6-0 at Swansea and 5-1 at home to Bury.

With two games left Saints had scored 89 goals. They then beat Swindon 5-1 at The Dell on 25th April, then two days later finished the season with a 6-1 home victory over Rotherham.

Saints ended the season in fifth place and their tally of 100 goals was easily the best in the Second Division. However, they conceded 73, more than all but six other teams.

FACT 40

1965
SOUTHAMPTON 9
WOLVES 3

The highest scoring game in which Southampton have ever been involved was on 18th September 1965. In a Second Division fixture at The Dell, there were twelve goals scored as the Saints beat Wolves 9-3.

Saints were behind in less than a minute when Tony Knapp headed into his own net. Martin Chivers equalised in the fourth minute and Sydenham put Saints ahead six minutes later. Almost immediately though Wolves equalised.

The home side took control in a devastating nine-minute spell either side of the half hour. Terry Paine rounded the keeper to restore the lead, then Chivers and George O'Brien set each other up for goals meaning Saints went into the interval 5-2 ahead.

Two minutes after the restart Jimmy Melia set up Chivers for his hat trick. Three minutes later Chivers made it 7-2, intercepting a weak back pass to score. Wolves pulled another one back but goals from John Sydenham and Paine put Saints 9-3 ahead with half an hour still to play. Amazingly there were no more goals but reports stated there could easily have been fourteen or fifteen for the home side.

It had been a massive statement of intent by Saints. They had thrashed a side who had just been relegated from the First Division and shown they were capable of getting there themselves.

FACT 41
1966
PROMOTED TO THE FIRST DIVISION

Southampton finished as runners up in the Second Division in 1965-66. They were unbeaten in their last twelve games to clinch promotion to English football's topflight for the first time in their history.

On 5th March Saints lost 1-0 at home to Birmingham, a defeat that left them in fifth place, four points behind the promotion spots. They followed this up by gaining a vital point in a 1-1 draw at fellow hopefuls Wolves.

Over Easter, Saints faced Bristol City, who were also in the hunt for promotion, home and away. Saints won 1-0 at Ashton Gate on Good Friday and drew 2-2 in the return at The Dell on Easter Monday.

Saints then picked up nine points out of a possible ten. After the final full round of fixtures on 7th May, they were in third place with two games still to play and promotion in their own hands.

On 9th May, Terry Paine's second half equaliser at Leyton Orient was the cause for huge celebrations amongst thousands of travelling Saints fans. They now knew that only a 6-0 defeat in their final game at already promoted Manchester City could deny their dream. Five days later at Maine Road the two teams played out a 0-0 draw and Saints were in the First Division.

FACT 42
1967
THE FOOTBALL LEAGUE'S TOP SCORER

Southampton finished nineteenth in their debut season in the First Division. Ron Davies was pivotal in their survival, finishing the season with 37 goals which made him the top scorer across all four divisions.

Saints paid £55,000 to Norwich for the Welsh international, who had never played in the First Division. Davies was noted for his heading ability and it was expected that he would take full advantage of the crosses provided by John Sydenham and Terry Paine.

Davies went on to show that there was far more to his game. He could turn an average cross into a good one with his ability to get to the ball and head it in the right direction. However, he could hold the ball, drop back to create play and had a capable left foot, with which he scored 23 of his 37 goals in 1966-67.

First Division survival had been secured before the last game of the season, in which Davies scored four in a 6-2 win against already relegated Aston Villa. The following season Davies got 28 goals, making him joint top First Division scorer alongside Manchester United's George Best.

Davies spent the best of his playing years at Saints, who rejected any offers from leading clubs. He joined Portsmouth in 1973 and eventually settled in the United States.

FACT 43
1969 INTER CITIES FAIRS CUP

Southampton appeared in European club competition for the first time in 1969-70. They reached the third round before losing on away goals to another English side.

Saints had finished seventh but the Inter Cities Fairs Cup didn't allow more than one team from the same city to enter. This meant they got into Europe at the expense of Everton and Tottenham.

In their first leg of the first round Saints suffered a shock 1-0 defeat at Norwegian amateurs Rosenborg BK. Back at The Dell, goals from Ron Davies and Terry Paine spared them an embarrassing exit.

Saints were again away in the first leg of the second round, against Portuguese side Vitoria Guimaraes. They twice came from behind to lead 3-2, but the home side equalised with two minutes to go. The home leg was much more one sided as Saints cruised to a 5-1 victory.

The third round was an all-English affair, as Saints were drawn against Newcastle United. The first leg at St James' Park ended 0-0 leaving the tie on a knife edge.

There was a crowd of over 25,000 at The Dell for the return game. Mick Channon gave Saints a first half lead but Pop Robson equalised after the break. It meant Newcastle went through on away goals, denying Saints a place in the quarter finals.

FACT 44
1969
THE DELL'S
RECORD ATTENDANCE

The highest attendance for a Southampton match at The Dell was on 8th October 1969. A crowd of 31,044 saw Saints lose 3-0 to a star-studded Manchester United side.

Earlier in the season, Saints had stunned United by winning 4-1 at Old Trafford. Despite this game at The Dell being midweek, a record crowd attended to see if United, European champions in 1968, could be beaten again.

Saints set out to stifle George Best and he was man marked by two defenders. This tactic worked for half an hour until he managed to break clear and run on to a through pass from Brian Kidd and smash the ball into the roof of the net.

Early in the second half Francis Burns added a second for United, who were ahead against the run of play. Just after the hour mark Bobby Charlton, a World Cup winner with England three years earlier, played a perfect pass for Kidd to make it 3-0.

The attendance of 31,044 broke a record at The Dell that had stood for twenty years. It was never equalled although Saints have had higher home crowds since moving to St Mary's in 2001.

FACT 45
1970
SIX WINS BUT STILL NOT RELEGATED

In 1969-70 Southampton won just six of their 42 games in the First Division. However, they avoided relegation thanks to the number of draws they picked up.

Saints won two out of their first six games, before going on a run of twenty games without a win. Eleven of those twenty games were draws and as only two points were awarded for a win, the points gained had far more value than today. It meant that after 26 games, Saints were actually fourth from bottom despite just two wins all season.

The winless run came to an end with a 2-1 win over Everton at The Dell on 17th January. This was the first of three successive wins that lifted them up one place in the table and five points clear of the drop zone.

Saints won just one of their last thirteen matches, a 3-1 win over Leeds at Elland Road on 28th March that ended the home side's title hopes. They lost their next two, but a 0-0 draw at home to Manchester City in their penultimate game confirmed their survival.

Saints finished the season in nineteenth, two places and three points clear of the relegation zone. Even under three points for a win Saints would have avoided the drop, although the margins would have been far tighter.

FACT 46
1973
MR SOUTHAMPTON
STEPS DOWN

Ted Bates stepped down as Southampton manager in November 1973. At the time he was the longest serving manager in the Football League, but it still wasn't the end of his association with Saints.

Between 1937 and 1953 Bates made 217 appearances as a player for Saints in a career that was interrupted by the Second World War. He remained as a coach and was appointed manager in 1955, taking Saints from the Third Division into Europe.

When Bates stepped aside as manager in November 1973 it was no surprise. It was part of a longer-term plan that involved the 55-year-old becoming chief executive and Lawrie McMenemy, who had been recruited as 'manager designate' in the summer, succeeding him as manager.

Even after he stepped back from day-to-day involvement, Bates remained as a director, vice-president and then president. In 2001, already dubbed "Mr Southampton", he was made a Freeman of the City. He also formally opened the new stadium, St Mary's.

By 2003 Bates's health was failing and he was too ill to attend Cardiff when Saints reached the FA Cup final. He died in November that year, having been involved with Saints for an amazing 66 years.

FACT 47
1974
NEW RELEGATION RULE HITS SOUTHAMPTON

In 1973-74 Southampton were the first victims of the new ruling that three clubs would be relegated from the First Division. Saints went down after finishing third bottom, which in previous seasons would have been enough to survive the drop.

Saints' relegation was even more frustrating as they had a reasonable start to the season. They were unbeaten in their first four games and in mid-December were fifth in the table.

However, Saints then had a terrible run, winning just 3 out of 22 games. During this run Saints lost ten away games in succession, meaning that on the final day of the season their fate was out of their hands. Norwich were already relegated, but Saints were in a battle with Manchester United, West Ham and Birmingham to avoid joining them. Saints needed to win at Everton and hope Birmingham or West Ham dropped points.

Saints task seemed a hopeless one against a side that had lost just once at home all season and had a chance of qualifying for Europe. However, they upset the form book by winning 3-0. It was in vain though as Birmingham won and West Ham drew, meaning Saints became the first team to go down as a result of three being relegated from the First Division.

FACT 48

1974
TEXACO CUP
RUNNERS UP

Southampton entered the Texaco Cup for the first time in 1974. They reached the final but were beaten over two legs by Newcastle United.

This was the fifth year of the sponsored competition that was open to English and Scottish clubs who hadn't qualified for Europe. Sixteen English teams had entered and were drawn into four groups, with the top sides progressing to quarter finals.

The group games were played before the league season started. Saints drew at Luton then beat West Ham and Orient to top their group. They then got the toughest possible quarter final draw, being paired with Rangers.

In front of over 35,000 at Ibrox, Saints won 3-1 thanks to two goals from Peter Osgood and one from Gerry O'Brien. They followed this up with a 2-0 win at The Dell to progress to the semi-finals, which were to be contested by four English sides. Saints beat Oldham 3-1 away then 2-1 at home to set up a final with Newcastle.

Saints were at home in the first leg on 27th November and won 1-0 thanks to a goal from David Armstrong. However, in the return at St James Park two weeks later they lost 3-0 after extra time. This turned out to be the last time the Texaco Cup was contested.

FACT 49
1976
FA CUP WINNERS

Southampton's only major trophy came in 1976 when they won the FA Cup. Second Division Saints stunned strong favourites Manchester United by beating them 1-0 in the final at Wembley.

Saints shocked topflight Aston Villa and West Bromwich Albion in the early rounds but were favourites themselves in the quarter and semi-finals. In the last eight they won 1-0 at Fourth Division Bradford City then beat Third Division Crystal Palace 2-0 in a semi-final at Stamford Bridge.

For the final United were the clear favourites, having finished third in the First Division. Early in the game they were the better side, but Stuart Pearson and Gerry Daly missed good opportunities. Saints keeper Ian Turner then did well to save a lob by Gordon Hill as their belief grew that if they remained determined, they could snatch victory.

Mick Channon was denied by United keeper Alex Stepney when one on one and Saints had a let off when Lou Macari headed against the bar. With seven minutes remaining Jim McCalliog played a perfect pass to Bobby Stokes whose shot gave Stepney no chance.

Saints held on for victory to win their first major trophy. Captain Peter Rodrigues was presented the cup by Queen Elizabeth II, the last time she attended an FA Cup final.

FACT 50

1976 ANGLO-ITALIAN LEAGUE CUP

Southampton featured in the last Anglo-Italian League Cup competition in 1976. They lost the two-legged final play off 4-1 on aggregate against Coppa Italia winners Napoli.

The short-lived competition began in 1969 and was played between the winners of the Coppa Italia and either the FA Cup or League Cup. It was not contested between 1972 and 1974 but revived in 1975.

Saints agreed to take part in 1976, with the first leg against Napoli taking place at The Dell on 21st September. The Italians were defensive in their approach and tough tackling on occasions. Mick Channon was closely marked by Bruscolotti who was rarely more than a few feet away from him.

After 67 minutes Saints finally found a way through when Channon managed to break free and cross for Steve Williams to score with a stunning volley. It was the eighteen-year old's first goal for Saints. Mel Blyth almost doubled the lead but his diving header came back off the post and it finished 1-0.

The second leg in Naples was on 15th November. Saints were already depleted due to injuries and were without Channon who was on international duty. Saints were well beaten by the home side, who ran out 4-0 winners in what turned out to be the last ever Anglo Italian League Cup game.

FACT 51
1977 EUROPEAN QUARTER FINALISTS

Southampton's best ever season in European competition was in 1976-77. Despite being a Second Division club, Saints reached the quarter finals of the European Cup Winners Cup.

Saints qualified as FA Cup winners and were drawn against French side Olympique Marseille in the first round. At The Dell, Saints built up a commanding first leg lead winning 4-0.

Although they were 1-0 down at half time in the second leg, David Peach scored a crucial away goal twenty minutes from time. Despite going on to lose 2-1 on the night, Saints had a comfortable aggregate victory.

The second round paired Saints against Carrick Rangers from Northern Ireland, who were at home in the first leg. Saints ran out 5-2 winners and finished the job at The Dell, winning 4-1 to set up a quarter final tie with the holders Anderlecht.

The first leg was in Brussels and Saints lost 2-0, leaving them with an uphill task in the return game. A penalty from Peach and strike from Ted McDougall levelled the tie, but François van der Elst's long range effort seven minutes from time ended Saints dreams of glory.

FACT 52
1977
BOBBY STOKES LEAVES

Bobby Stokes, the scorer of the most famous goal in Southampton's history, left the club just a year later.

Originally from Portsmouth, Stokes failed a trial with his hometown club as a schoolboy. He became an apprentice with Saints and scored twice on his debut against Burnley as an eighteen-year-old in April 1969.

At the start of the FA Cup winning season Stokes asked for a transfer but chose against a move to Portsmouth, the only club to show an interest. He announced his intention to stay following the Wembley triumph but the arrival of Ted McDougall and Alan Ball meant his opportunities became limited.

After just one goal in eleven appearances during 1976-77 Stokes did sign for Portsmouth. He scored just twice in 24 games there before having loan spells with non-league Waterlooville and Cheltenham, then North American Soccer League side Washington Diplomats.

Stokes drifted out of the game, and in the 1980s ran a pub and later a café near Portsmouth Harbour. He died in 1995 at the age of just 44 after contracting bronchial pneumonia.

FACT 53
1978
DOUBLE
PROMOTION PARTY

There were double promotion celebrations at The Dell on 29th April 1978. Southampton drew 0-0 with Tottenham, a result that ensured both teams went up to the First Division.

Saints maintained a remarkable consistency throughout the season but the promotion race was an extremely tight battle with three other clubs; Bolton, Tottenham and Brighton.

Going into the last day of the season, Bolton were already up and Saints were virtually certain of promotion due to their superior goal difference. In an added twist, Saints and Tottenham were due to face each other at The Dell. A draw would see both sides go up providing Brighton didn't win their last game by eleven goals. Saints spent £6,000 providing extra segregation measures at the ground and all pubs in the city were closed before the game.

The game, watched by a crowd of almost 29,000 was not a classic, but the two sides could not be accused of playing out a draw to deny Brighton. Saints wanted to finish as champions and Tony Funnell went close three times in the first half, including hitting the post.

After the match champagne flowed in both dressing rooms as they celebrated a return to the First Division. It had been a four-year absence for Saints and one year for Tottenham.

FACT 54

1979 LEAGUE CUP FINALISTS

Southampton reached the final of the League Cup for the first time in 1978-79. They were left disappointed though after losing 3-2 to Nottingham Forest.

With the exception of Fourth Division Reading in the last sixteen, Saints were drawn against fellow topflight opposition at every stage of the competition. After knocking out Birmingham, Derby, Manchester City and Leeds, their opponents at Wembley were Forest, reigning Football League champions and League Cup holders.

The game was fifteen minutes old when David Peach played a one-two with Alan Ball before rounding Peter Shilton to score for Saints. For the remainder of the half Saints defence coped well with any pressure and Ball was in command of the midfield.

After half time Forest upped the pace and equalised after just five minutes when Chris Nicholl's attempted block of a cross only fell into the path of Gary Birtles to score. Saints held on until the 77th minute when Birtles got his second after being set up by Tony Woodcock, who scored himself five minutes later to end Saints dreams of glory.

With three minutes remaining Nick Holmes scored for Saints with an unstoppable shot but there was no miracle comeback. There was no shame in defeat for Saints though against a side that also won the European Cup that season.

FACT 55
1980
KEVIN KEEGAN

Southampton stunned the football world in 1980 when they agreed a deal to sign Kevin Keegan, twice a European Footballer of the Year.

Keegan, a European Cup winner with Liverpool, had moved to Hamburg in 1977, winning the coveted European award in 1978 and 1979. In February 1980, Lawrie McMenemy invited journalists to a press conference where it was announced he would be joining Saints at the end of the season.

Keegan was still only 28 years old and it was a huge coup for Saints. McMenemy described it as a greater achievement than winning the FA Cup, as it amounted to progress that they could attract such a top-quality player. The cost of signing him was easily recouped by season ticket sales.

In his first season Keegan was the club's leading scorer. This was despite injury limiting him to 27 starts as Saints qualified for Europe by finishing sixth, their highest league position to date.

The following season Keegan missed just one game as Saints challenged for the title before fading away at the end of the season. However, he had a falling out with McMenemy and opted to leave in the summer, signing for Second Division Newcastle. In eighty appearances for Saints, he had scored 42 goals.

FACT 56
1982
FIRST TO SEVENTH

Southampton had hopes of winning the Football League Championship in 1981-82. However, after leading the way for two months until late March, they had a poor run at the end and finished seventh.

There was no sign of things to come at the end of October when Saints were in tenth place with five wins, five defeats and a goal difference of minus one. A run of one defeat in ten games saw Saints slowly climb the table and they hit the top on 30th January after a 1-0 win at Middlesbrough.

Saints remained unbeaten for three more games but then lost 5-2 at Ipswich. It was now very tight at the top and postponements caused by a severe winter meant all of Saints rivals had games in hand. They remained at the top for their next six games but dropped to second after a defeat at Tottenham on 20th March.

On 10th April Saints lost 3-0 to Aston Villa at The Dell, meaning they fell to fifth. They were now seven points behind leaders Liverpool, having played two games more. They eventually finished in seventh, having won only three and losing five of their last ten games.

FACT 57
1982
MICK CHANNON
LEAVES AGAIN

Southampton's all-time record goalscorer is Mick Channon, who scored 228 goals in 607 appearances. He signed professional forms for Saints in 1965 and left for the second time in 1982, having spent two seasons at Manchester City in the late 1970s.

Channon made his debut for Saints as a seventeen-year-old in 1966 and his trademark windmill goal celebration and West Country accent made him a familiar figure throughout the land. He earned the first of his 46 England caps in 1972 and stayed at Saints after relegation in 1974 even though he was now an established international.

In 1976 he played a part in the goal that won Saints the FA Cup but the following year joined Manchester City, who had just finished runners up to Liverpool in the First Division.

Channon struggled at City and he re-joined Saints, now back in the top flight, in 1979. Although his goal ratio dropped, his last one against Liverpool in April 1982 was truly special. A sixteen-pass move involving eight players was finished off by Channon and voted goal of the season on BBC's Match of the Day.

After being released in 1982, Channon continued playing for five more years. He then became a successful racehorse trainer and has a hospitality suite named after him at St Mary's.

FACT 58
1984
DOUBLE DISAPPOINTMENT

Southampton enjoyed arguably their best ever season in 1983-84. They finished second to Liverpool in the First Division and also went close in the FA Cup, reaching the semi-final.

Saints enjoyed a good start to the campaign, remaining unbeaten for their first six games. These included a 1-1 draw at Liverpool and 3-0 victory over Manchester United at The Dell. However, a run of three wins from nine saw them drop down to eighth in the table.

Form picked up over the winter period and on 16th March Saints enjoyed a memorable 2-0 home win over Liverpool, Danny Wallace scoring with a stunning overhead kick. Saints were now nine points off the top, but with two games in hand on all three sides above them.

Saints then drew one and lost two of their next three league games, all but ending their title hopes. There was then disappointment in the FA Cup when they lost 1-0 against Everton at Arsenal's Highbury Stadium.

Despite their dreams of a double being gone, Saints refused to let their heads drop. They were unbeaten in their last nine games of the season in which there were memorable wins at The Dell over Coventry (8-2) and Tottenham (5-0). It meant Saints finished in second place, just three points behind Liverpool.

FACT 59

1985
LAWRIE McMENEMY QUITS

Southampton's most successful manager Lawrie McMenemy resigned from his role in 1985. However, it was not the end of his association with the club and he was later back in other capacities.

McMenemy was just 37 years old when he succeeded Ted Bates as manager in 1973. Despite relegation that season, the Board stuck with him.

In 1976 McMenemy led Second Division Saints to their greatest triumph, victory in the FA Cup final over Manchester United. Two years later he secured promotion back to the topflight and the following year Saints were finalists in the League Cup.

McMenemy attracted a number of high-profile internationals to the club. Kevin Keegan was the most notable but he also signed veteran England World Cup winner Alan Ball and the country's top keeper, Peter Shilton. This blend of youth and experience helped Saints to a second-place finish in 1984 and fifth a year later.

On 1st June McMenemy resigned, issuing a statement which said, "I have not been satisfied with the job for the last two years, I think I have explored all the avenues with this club."

Later that summer McMenemy was appointed as manager of relegated Sunderland. He was back at Saints in the 1990s as Director of Football and in 2006 was appointed as a non-executive director.

FACT 60
1985
SCREEN SPORT
SUPER CUP

Southampton were unable to take part in Europe in 1985-6 due to all English clubs being banned. Instead, they competed in the Screen Sport Super Cup along with the five other English clubs denied European competition.

In May 1985, 39 Juventus fans were killed when a wall collapsed following a charge by Liverpool fans prior to the 1985 European Cup final in Brussels. UEFA acted by banning all English clubs indefinitely from their competitions.

To make up for lost revenue, a competition was organised for the six English clubs who would have been in Europe. They were split into two groups of three, playing each other twice with the top two progressing to the semi-finals. The competition was sponsored by satellite television company Screen Sport, who broadcast all of the games.

Saints helped get the competition started on 17th September, when they lost 2-1 at Liverpool. Two weeks later they lost 2-1 again, this time at Tottenham. In their first home game, Saints drew 1-1 with Liverpool, meaning they still had a chance of progressing. However, they were then beaten 3-1 by Spurs, confirming they would finish bottom of the group.

The competition was so ill thought of that the final between Liverpool and Everton was carried over until the following season, and it was never contested again.

FACT 61

1987
FIRST TOPFLIGHT
SOUTH COAST DERBY

Southampton and Portsmouth met for the first time in the topflight on 22nd August 1987. In an entertaining game at Fratton Park, the two sides drew 2-2 in the First Division fixture.

Portsmouth were back in the top division after an absence of 28 years. They had lost their opening two matches, while Saints had started with a win and a draw.

After twenty minutes Saints keeper Tim Flowers and left back Derek Statham had a mix-up and Vince Hilaire stole in to score for the home side. Saints were level five minutes later when Colin Clarke's shot bounced into the net off the keeper Alan Knight.

Saints took the lead three minutes after half time. Clarke was on target again, scoring after a one-two with Gordon Hobson. Saints were unable to hold on for victory, with Portsmouth levelling sixteen minutes from time. Clive Whitehead bundled the ball into the net after it had been headed down by Ian Baird.

In the return fixture in January Portsmouth won 2-0 at The Dell. They were relegated at the end of the season and the two sides didn't meet again in the league until 2003-04.

FACT 62
1988
YOUNGEST FOOTBALL LEAGUE HAT TRICK

History was made when Southampton beat Arsenal 4-2 on 9th April 1988. Alan Shearer became the youngest player to score a hat trick in the Football League at the age of 17 years and 240 days.

Shearer had been with Saints youth academy since 1986. He had already made two substitute appearances but was given an opportunity to start this game when Danny Wallace was ruled out with an ankle injury.

It took Shearer just five minutes to open the scoring, heading in a ball from Graham Baker. Arsenal equalised through Kevin Bond's own goal but after 32 minutes Saints went back ahead with Shearer starting and finishing the move.

Mark Blake made it 3-1 before half time then in the 49th minute Shearer completed his hat trick, scoring the rebound after his first effort hit the bar. Paul Davis scored a consolation for the visitors before Shearer was substituted to a standing ovation. He had broken a thirty-year record previously held by Jimmy Greaves for the youngest hat trick scorer.

In the summer Shearer was offered a full-time contract that significantly increased his £35 a week wages. He was then eased into a regular role in the team, becoming an England international in 1992. That summer he was sold to Blackburn for £3.6 million, a new British transfer record.

FACT 63 — 1988
THE WALLACE BROTHERS

History was made when Southampton played Sheffield Wednesday at The Dell on 22nd October 1988. For the first time in 67 years three brothers appeared on the same side in a First Division fixture.

The eldest of the Wallace brothers, Danny, was born in 1964 and established himself in the Saints side as a winger in 1982-83. Twins Ray and Rod were five years younger, with Rod making the breakthrough as a striker in 1987-88.

Ray, a full back, came into the first team picture the following season and replaced Gerry Forrest in the starting line-up for the game against Wednesday. In the nineteenth minute the three brothers were almost involved in a dream goal. Danny released Ray down the right flank, but his cross towards Rod was intercepted by Wednesday defender Mel Sterland.

Five minutes before half time Rod was brought down in the area and Derek Statham dispatched the penalty. However Wednesday hit back to win the game 2-1 and spoil their day.

The three brothers were regulars for the rest of the season but Danny was sold to Manchester United in the summer of 1989. Over the next two seasons Rod featured far more than Ray and in the summer of 1991 the twins were sold to Leeds in a combined deal worth £1.6 million.

FACT 64

1992 FULL MEMBERS CUP FINALISTS

Southampton appeared at Wembley for the first time in thirteen years when they reached the final of the Full Members Cup in 1992. By coincidence their opponents were Nottingham Forest, the same as in 1979, and like then the game ended in a 3-2 defeat for Saints.

The Full Members Cup was inaugurated in 1985 and was an optional tournament for clubs in the top two divisions. This was Saints' fifth appearance but first time they had made it past the opening two rounds.

Although the competition was not popular in the early stages, a final at Wembley was always a special event and Saints fans made up half of the 67,888 attendance.

Forest went ahead through Scott Gemmill's strike after fourteen minutes and shortly before half time Kingsley Black doubled their lead. In the 64th minute Matt Le Tissier's header from a Neil Ruddock cross pulled one back and twenty minutes later Kevin Moore headed in a corner to bring Saints level.

Saints were the better side for the rest of the game and looked the more likely winners but couldn't find a way through. It looked to be heading to penalties but Gemmill scored Forest's winner five minutes before the end of extra time.

FACT 65
1994
SMALLEST STADIUM IN PREMIER LEAGUE

In 1994 the conversion of The Dell to an all-seated stadium made it the smallest in the Premier League. It's capacity of 15,352 was just two-thirds of what it had been in the 1980s.

Following the Hillsborough Disaster of 1989, in which 96 Liverpool fans were killed at an FA Cup semi-final in Sheffield, the government introduced legislation meaning that topflight stadiums had to be all seated by 1994.

Throughout the 1980s The Dell had a capacity of 25,000 of which 9,175 were seats. Due to it being so hemmed in, expansion was impossible but a proposed move to Stonham failed to materialise.

The first end to be roofed and seated was the Archers Road terrace. This was so shallow that it contained just 1,299 seats when completed. In 1994 the Milton Road end posed a much bigger challenge due to its angled nature. Local architects WH Saunders & Sons developed what Simon Inglis described in *The Football Grounds of Great Britain* as "An unnerving collection of angles, all appearing different from various parts of the ground."

The new Milton Road stand, with a goalpost style roof, sat 2,897. With a total capacity of 15,352, Saints were generating far less in matchday revenue than their Premier League rivals.

FACT 66

1995
A SEASON
OF DRAWS

Southampton set a Premier League record for drawn games in 1994-95. They drew eighteen of their 42 matches, including one sequence of seven in a row.

Saints started the season off with two 1-1 draws, at home to Blackburn and away to Aston Villa. They then lost two in succession but won four out of five, the other being drawn, to climb to seventh by mid-October.

Three straight defeats followed before Saints drew three out of four in November. During December they won one and lost three. A 2-2 draw at QPR on 28th December started the run of seven successive draws. Only two of these were at home and both finished 2-2, against Manchester City and Manchester United. The away draws were at Sheffield Wednesday (1-1), Leeds United (0-0), Arsenal (1-1) and Norwich City (2-2).

The seven-game sequence was ended with a 2-1 defeat at Ipswich before two more draws followed, leaving Saints in the relegation zone. Five wins from six lifted them clear and the season ended on 14th May with another draw, 2-2 against Leicester at The Dell.

Of Saints' other 24 fixtures, they won twelve and lost twelve. No other team in the Premier League has drawn eighteen games over the season while the record of seven in succession is shared by two other clubs.

FACT 67
1995
HAT TRICK
DOUBLE DEFEAT

Matt Le Tissier's scoring feats have earned him an unusual record. He is the only Premier League player to end up on the losing side twice whilst scoring a hat trick.

The first occasion was against Oldham on the last day of the 1992-93 season. Le Tissier hit a hat trick in a game that Oldham won 4-3 to avoid relegation.

Le Tissier's second unlucky hat trick was against Nottingham Forest at The Dell on the opening day of 1995-96. It was a game that also finished 4-3.

Saints trailed after eight minutes when Colin Cooper scored a curling free kick. Within a minute Saints were level after being awarded a penalty for a foul by Steve Chettle on Le Tissier, who got back up to score from the spot.

By half time Forest led 3-1 thanks to goals from Ian Woan and Bryan Roy. Twenty minutes into the second half Saints were awarded another penalty when Le Tissier was bundled over by Lars Bohinen. Le Tissier coolly converted the kick.

Saints were dealt a further blow when Roy extended Forest's lead with eleven minutes remaining. Two minutes later Le Tissier gave Saints hope again from another dead ball situation. This time it was a free kick from twenty yards which he drove low into the net but Saints were unable to find an equaliser.

FACT 68
1996
STAYING UP AT EXPENSE OF FORMER BOSS

Southampton narrowly avoided relegation in 1995-96. Only goal difference kept them above Manchester City, managed by Alan Ball who had left the Saints in acrimonious circumstances during the close season.

Ball had become Saints' boss in January 1994. After avoiding the drop that season and a mid-table finish in 1994-95 he was rewarded with a new three-year contract. However, to the dismay of Saints fans he was reluctantly allowed to depart for Manchester City, who he believed had more ambition.

Reserve manager Dave Merrington was promoted to take charge of the first team. Saints and City struggled all season and going into the final day were battling with Coventry to avoid relegation. All three sides were level on points, with Saints and Coventry having a superior goal difference.

Saints and Coventry drew 0-0 at home to Wimbledon and Leeds respectively. At Maine Road, City came from 2-0 down against Liverpool to be drawing 2-2 with ten minutes remaining. Ball then wrongly heard that Saints were losing and instructed his players to keep the ball by the corner flag, a disastrous instruction that took City down and kept Saints up.

Avoiding relegation failed to save Merrington from the sack and he was replaced that summer by Graeme Souness. Ball was dismissed by City early the following season.

FACT 69

1996
DOUBLE TROUBLE
FOR UNITED

Southampton twice enjoyed convincing wins over Manchester United in 1996. The first of these was blamed by United manager Alex Ferguson on the colour of their shirts, but he could offer no excuses for the second.

When United came to The Dell on 13th April Saints were in a relegation battle. However, in a sensational first half, Saints stormed into a 3-0 lead thanks to goals from Ken Monkou, Neil Shipperley and Matt Le Tissier.

For the second half United came out wearing a different strip, having changed from grey shirts to blue and white. Saints held out and didn't concede a consolation until a minute from full time. Afterwards, Ferguson said that in the first half the players were unable to pick each other out due to the grey shirts.

Saints avoided relegation and United were back at The Dell on 26th October. Goals from Eyal Berkovic, Matt Le Tissier and Egil Østenstad gave Saints a 3-1 half time lead, with United down to ten men due to Roy Keane's sending off.

Early in the second half United pulled a goal back but Berkovic and Østenstad extended Saints' lead to 5-2. United got back to 5-3 but a Gary Neville own goal meant it finished 6-3 to Saints. This time, Ferguson couldn't blame the defeat on anything.

FACT 70
1996
ALI DIA

One of the strangest signings in Southampton history was Ali Dia. During an injury crisis in 1996, manager Graeme Souness took the chance on the Senegalese player but it later transpired Souness had been duped by a hoax phone call.

Souness was persuaded to give Dia a trial by his agent, who claimed to be Liberian superstar and former AC Milan player George Weah. Due to an injury crisis Dia was on the bench for a home game against Leeds on 23rd November despite having taken part in just one training session.

After twenty minutes Matt Le Tissier picked up an injury and with no other strikers available, Souness sent Dia on. To say he failed to impress was an understatement and he was substituted himself late in a game that Saints lost 2-0.

Dia was quickly released from his trial and further investigations established that the man claiming to be Weah had been calling several clubs with the recommendation.

Le Tissier told the *Guardian* twenty years later, "His performance was almost comical. He kind of took my place, but he didn't really have a position. He was just wandering everywhere. I don't think he realised what position he was supposed to be in. In the end he got himself subbed because he was that bad."

FACT 71

1997
FRANCIS BENALI'S
ONLY GOAL

Southampton cult legend Francis Benali played 369 games for the club between 1988 and 2003. However, the one-time striker scored just one goal, against Leicester on 13th December 1997.

Benali was a striker in his teenage years before starting his Saints career in midfield for the reserves. When he made his debut as a substitute in 1988, it was at left back and apart from occasional spells in central defence, that was where he stayed for the rest of his career.

During his eventful Saints career, Benali picked up eleven red cards and made a number of crucial goal line clearances but rarely crossed the halfway line. However, one occasion that he did was when Saints were awarded a second half free kick in his 287th appearance against Leicester at The Dell.

Matt Le Tissier picked out Benali who met the ball perfectly to power an unstoppable header past Kasey Keller. As the crowd screamed with joy, Benali stood there soaking up the adulation. He later said, "I just stood there and listened, I have practised this moment for years."

Benali left Saints in 2003. He has since become a club ambassador, media pundit and raised hundreds of thousands of pounds for charity by doing cycling and running challenges.

FACT 72

1999
THE
GREAT ESCAPE

Southampton endured a terrible season in 1998-99 and looked doomed to relegation. However, they won their last three games to avoid the drop at the expense of Charlton.

Saints lost their opening five games, including a humiliating 5-0 defeat against Charlton at The Valley. They won just three times before New Year, leaving them second to bottom with twenty games played.

From January form gradually improved, especially at The Dell where they won five successive matches. Away form remained dire however. This meant that at the end of April, Saints remained in the relegation zone with just three games remaining. The first of these was at home to Leicester on 1st May, with Saints winning 2-1 thanks to goals from Chris Marsden and James Beattie. This lifted Saints out of the bottom three for the first time that season.

The following week 10,000 Saints cheered their side to a 2-0 win over Wimbledon at Selhurst Park. Matt Le Tissier came off the bench to set up Beattie for the opening goal then scored directly from a corner.

The last match of the season was at home to Everton, with Saints' fate remaining in their own hands. Marian Pahars scored twice in a 2-0 win to complete a remarkable escape a week after planning permission had been granted for a new 32,000 seat stadium.

FACT 73
2001
GOODBYE
TO THE DELL

Southampton left their home of 103 years at the end of 2000-01. As homely as it was, The Dell simply wasn't a sustainable venue for a Premier League club.

Saints had been looking to move since the mid-nineties but a proposal to relocate to Eastleigh fell through. In 1999 plans were approved for a new 32,000 capacity stadium off Britannia Road next to the River Itchen, with a build time of two years.

The last competitive game at The Dell was against Arsenal on 19th May 2001. In a carnival atmosphere, Hasan Kachloul twice equalised after strikes from the Gunners. Then with a minute remaining, Matt Le Tissier scored a spectacular volley to give Saints a 3-2 victory.

On 26th May, Saints played Brighton & Hove Albion in a friendly, a tribute to the fact it was a precursor club, Brighton United, who had been the first opponents there. Uwe Rosler scored the only goal as Saints won 1-0, then afterwards fans were invited to strip away seating.

Apartment blocks now stand on the site, but the Saints connection remains as they are named after former players: Stokes Court, Ted Bates Court, Le Tissier Court, Channon Court, Wallace Court.

FACT 74

2001
ST MARY'S

Just over two months after the last match at The Dell, Southampton played their first game at their new home. Spanish side Espanyol provided the opposition for a friendly on 1st August 2001.

The stadium, which tends to be referred to simply as St Mary's, took just twenty months to complete after construction started in December 1999. The concrete bowl seats just over 32,000, with all four stands being of equal height and named after the areas they face.

Espanyol were the opposition for the first game, with the *Daily Echo* reporting that Saints fans "stood open mouthed in wonder at the magnificence of their new stadium."

The first half of the opening game was certainly one to forget. Matt Le Tissier looked certain to score the first goal there but mistimed his kick. Martin Posse then put Espanyol ahead with an acrobatic volley after eight minutes. Saints were ripped apart by the La Liga side who raced into a 4-0 lead at the break.

Saints were much better in the second half. Kevin Davies pulled a goal back after 55 minutes then Uwe Rosler scored twice to give the score line a respectable look.

St Mary's has the potential to be expanded to a capacity of 50,000. It has hosted four England internationals and also a number of high-profile rock concerts.

FACT 75
2002
'LE TISS' RETIRES

Matt Le Tissier, arguably Southampton's greatest ever player, retired from professional football in 2002. He had spent sixteen years at the club, resisting opportunities to move elsewhere.

'Le Tiss', or 'Le God', as he was commonly known, was from Guernsey in the Channel Islands and signed professional forms in October 1986 around the time of his eighteenth birthday. That season he scored twice as Saints beat Manchester United 4-1 in the League Cup and also a hat trick against Leicester in the league.

Playing as an attacking midfielder, Le Tissier gained a reputation for the spectacular. Against Newcastle in 1993-94, he scored an outrageous goal by using his heel to control a misplaced header, volleying the ball past one defender, half volleying it past another then placing it past the keeper.

In 1994-95 he won the goal of the season award for a forty-yard chip against Blackburn. Throughout the 1990s his goals kept Saints in the Premier League but he was never tempted by offers from elsewhere. It was a travesty that he featured only eight times for England.

Le Tissier announced his retirement towards the end of 2001-02 when he suffered a recurring calf strain. In total he had played 462 times for Saints, scoring 209 goals. He then had two seasons as a semi-professional with Eastleigh, playing in the Southern League.

FACT 76

2003
SAINTS LOSE FIRST INDOOR FA CUP FINAL

In 2003 Southampton reached the FA Cup final for the first time since winning the competition in 1976. There was to be no glory for Saints though, as they were beaten 1-0 by Arsenal with the roof closed at Cardiff's Millennium Stadium.

Saints beat Tottenham, Millwall, Norwich, Wolverhampton and Watford 2-1 to set up a clash with Arsenal in Cardiff, where finals were played whilst Wembley was being rebuilt.

Due to heavy rain the night before and more showers forecast on match day, the decision was made to close the roof. Saints were without injured striker Marian Pahars and also had problems in defence, leading to manager Gordon Strachan handing 21-year-old right back Chris Baird his first start.

Despite his inexperience, Baird didn't look out of place, making a goal line clearance and going close with a curling shot. In the 38th minute Robert Pires gave Arsenal the lead and only poor finishing prevented them extending this before the break.

Both sides had their chances in the second half. James Beattie went agonisingly close for Saints in injury time when his goal bound header was cleared by Ashley Cole. Soon after the final whistle blew and Strachan said of his players, "I'm very proud of the way they competed. I couldn't have asked for anymore."

FACT 77
2003
DISAPPOINTMENT ON EUROPEAN RETURN

In 2003-04 Southampton's first European campaign in nineteen seasons ended in disappointment. They were beaten over two legs by Romanians Steaua Bucharest in the first round of the UEFA Cup.

The home leg attracted a capacity crowd to St Mary's, but they were stunned when the visitors went ahead midway through the first half. Steaua then defended deep, frustrating Saints who had plenty of possession but couldn't find any openings. In the second half Kevin Phillips took advantage of a poor back pass to make it 1-1 but they failed to find the winning goal.

Due to the away goals rule Saints needed to score in the second leg to have any chance of progressing. Despite a hostile home crowd at the Ghencea Stadium, Saints had the better of the first half. Phillips twice went close, heading over the bar and having his shot saved when one on one with the keeper.

The second half was the same as the first, with Saints dominating the game. Rory Delap just failed to connect with a knock down by James Beattie and Anders Svensson's long range effort went just past the post. However, as the game went on and Saints tired, Steaua became more adventurous and delivered a knockout blow when Claudiu Răducanu scored eight minutes from time.

FACT 78

2005
EX POMPEY BOSS TAKES SOUTHAMPTON DOWN

Southampton were relegated from the Premier League in 2004-05 after 27 years in the topflight. They sensationally turned to Portsmouth's manager Harry Redknapp in a bid to avoid the drop but went down following defeat on the last day of the season.

Manager Paul Sturrock left by mutual consent after just two games of the season. He was replaced by academy coach Steve Wigley, who won just one of his fourteen games in charge before being sacked on 8th December.

Saints then stunned the football world by appointing Redknapp, who had resigned as Portsmouth boss two weeks earlier saying he needed a break from the game.

After a slow start results picked up in February when Saints went five games unbeaten. On 30th April they lifted themselves out of the bottom three with a 4-3 home win over fellow strugglers Norwich City. They then drew 2-2 at Crystal Palace, another side who were battling relegation.

On the final day of the season Saints fate was in their own hands. A win over Manchester United at St Mary's would guarantee survival and after ten minutes they were on course thanks to a John O'Shea own goal. United hit back to win 2-1 and results elsewhere condemned Saints to a bottom place finish and second tier football for the first time since 1978.

FACT 79
2005
CROUCHIE'S INJURY TIME
CUP DERBY WINNER

Harry Redknapp's decision to leave Portsmouth for Southampton was given an added twist when the two sides were drawn against each other in the FA Cup. In a fiery fourth round encounter at St Mary's, Saints won thanks to Peter Crouch's injury time penalty.

Redknapp had been in charge of Saints less than two months when the two rivals met on 29th January. Both sides wasted first half chances but it was Saints who broke the deadlock after 54 minutes, Matt Oakley collecting a pass from Michael Svensson to score from twenty yards. Within three minutes though Portsmouth were level, Yakubu converting the penalty after Claus Lundekvam's foul on Diomansy Kamara.

Danny Higginbotham thought he had restored Saints lead but his strike was ruled out for offside. Kamara was then sent off for a second yellow card when he needlessly handballed. Portsmouth had a great opportunity to win the game with seven minutes left but Ricardo Fuller fired over from seven yards.

In injury time, Matt Taylor appeared to handle a cross but it took a long time for the referee and his assistant to award a spot kick. After what seemed an eternity, Crouch held his nerve to slot the ball home and take Saints into the next round.

FACT 80

2005
YOUNGEST PLAYER

On the opening day of the 2005-06 season, Theo Walcott became Southampton's youngest ever player. Aged just 16 years and 143 days, he went on as a second half substitute during a 0-0 draw with Wolverhampton Wanderers at St Mary's.

Walcott had been a member of the side that lost the previous season's FA Youth Cup final against Ipswich Town. During the campaign he had become Saints' youngest ever reserve player. Just two weeks after leaving school, he was included in a pre-season trip to Scotland and named on the bench for the first game of the new campaign on 6th August. With seventeen minutes remaining, he replaced Kenwynne Jones.

Two months later Walcott made his first start for Saints, scoring in a 2-1 defeat at Leeds. However, before he had even reached his seventeenth birthday he had been signed by Arsenal for an initial payment of £5 million. In the summer he was sensationally included in the England World Cup squad, despite not making a Premier League appearance at that point.

Walcott remained at Arsenal for twelve years before moving to Everton. Things came full circle for him in October 2020 when at the age of 31, he re-joined Saints on a season long loan.

FACT 81

2007 PLAYOFF DISAPPOINTMENT

In their quest to return to the Premier League, Southampton sneaked into the playoffs at the end of the 2005-06 season. However, they were disappointed after losing on penalties to Derby County in their semi-final.

After finishing twelfth in 2005-06, the following season was better, but Saints remained inconsistent and only made it into the playoffs by one point after winning their last three games.

Against Derby at St Mary's on 12th May, Andrew Surman gave Saints an early lead, but Derby hit back to win 2-1, leaving Saints with an uphill task to reach the final. At Pride Park, Saints fell behind after just three minutes but Jhon Viafara quickly made it 1-1. Nine minutes into the second half Viafara levelled the tie with a fierce shot, only for Leon Best to score an own goal by slicing a clearance past his keeper.

With a minute remaining Grzegorz Rasiak scored for Saints to force extra time. There was no further scoring and with away goals not counting as double, a penalty shoot-out was needed.

The unfortunate Best fired the first spot kick wide. The next seven kicks were all converted meaning that Iñigo Idiakez had to score Saints' fifth penalty. He shot wide and Saints hopes of a return to the Premier League were over.

FACT 82
2008
SAINTS SAVED BY
FAVOURABLE RESULTS

After missing out on promotion via the playoffs, the following season turned into a huge disappointment for Southampton. They had three different managers during 2007-08 and only avoided the drop thanks to favourable results on the last day of the season.

Form was again indifferent, but Saints were still closer in terms of points to the playoffs than relegation places in the middle of January. However, the resignation of manager George Burley to take the Scotland job had a huge detrimental effect.

John Gorman took over as caretaker manager and picked up one point from four games in charge. In February Nigel Pearson took over but just two wins in twelve games meant Saints fell into the bottom three. It meant in their last game Saints knew they had to beat Sheffield United at St Mary's and hope other results went their way.

Saints looked to be heading to League One when they trailed 1-0 after 23 minutes but came back to lead 2-1. United equalised but after 69 minutes Stern John restored the lead, only to receive a red card with ten minutes to go. Saints did hold on and condemned Leicester City to the drop. Pearson's contract wasn't renewed and he was replaced by Jan Poortvliet.

FACT 83

2009
DOWN TO LEAGUE ONE

There was to be no last day escape from relegation for Southampton in 2008-09. They were never out of the drop zone after Christmas and their relegation was confirmed in the penultimate game of the season.

Dutchman Jan Poortvliet was appointed manager in the summer despite having never played or managed in England. He was Saints tenth boss in as many years and the first from outside the British Isles. Saints lost four of their first five games and were in and out of the bottom three during the first half of the season.

Four straight defeats in December saw Saints fall back into the relegation zone and after a 2-1 home defeat to Doncaster on 23rd January, Poortvliet resigned as manager. He was replaced by his youth academy coach Mark Wotte, who was also Dutch.

Wotte failed to win any of his first four games but three straight wins gave them a fighting chance. However, this was followed by a dreadful seven game winless run that left Saints on the brink.

On 25th April, Saints twice surrendered the lead in a 2-2 draw with Burnley at St Mary's in their last home game of the season. They also knew that the road back up would be harder because of a ten-point deduction imposed due to going into administration.

FACT 84
2009
ADMINISTRATION

Southampton's financial problems meant they were placed into administration in 2009. This led to the club being deducted ten points but thankfully a buyer was found and they could look forward with optimism.

In April that year Southampton Leisure Holdings, the club's parent company, entered administration. The search for a buyer was relatively short and in July it was confirmed that Swiss businessman Markus Liebherr, who owned a number of engineering companies, had bought the club.

A statement by the administrators said that Liebherr had been attracted by the club's "rich sporting heritage, loyal fan base, first class stadium and training facilities and the potential for the Saints to regain their rightful place at the higher echelons of English football."

Patience would be required though as administration meant Saints started 2009-10 on minus ten points. With Alan Pardew appointed as manager in place of Mark Wotte, they started the season slowly and failed to win any of their first seven games.

Saints finally climbed out of the relegation zone at the beginning of December and never looked back. They lost just three of their last 22 games but it was not quite enough to make the playoffs. They finished in seventh place but would have been fifth, just three points off an automatic promotion place, had it not been for the deduction.

FACT 85
2010 FOOTBALL LEAGUE TROPHY WINNERS

In 2009-10 Southampton won the Football League Trophy. It was the club's first silverware since winning the FA Cup in 1976 and was a huge boost after two relegations and administration in the previous five years.

Saints beat Torquay United, Charlton Athletic, Norwich City and MK Dons to reach the final, where the opponents were Carlisle United. With a promotion push looking unlikely due to the ten-point deduction imposed after administration, it was a welcome diversion for fans and 44,000 tickets were sold for Saints' first appearance at the new Wembley.

With a quarter of an hour gone, Rickie Lambert gave Saints the lead after they were awarded a penalty for a handball. Adam Lallana doubled the advantage with a header shortly before half time. Five minutes into the second half Papa Waigo made it 3-0, heading into an empty net after Michail Antonio's effort was saved.

On the hour mark Antonio scored Saints fourth from the edge of the area. The rest of the game was played out at a slow pace with Carlisle getting a consolation seven minutes from time.

The occasion may not have been as significant as in 1976, but it was one to cherish for fans, being a clear marker that Saints were on their way back after the most turbulent period in the club's history.

FACT 86

2011
PROMOTED FROM LEAGUE ONE

In 2010-11 an early season managerial change brought about an upturn in Southampton's fortunes. It led to them finishing in second place and securing automatic promotion.

After just one win in the opening three games Alan Pardew was sacked at the end of August. His assistant Dean Wilkins took over and lost both his games in charge before being replaced by Nigel Adkins, who had twice taken Scunthorpe into the Championship.

Adkins lost his first game 2-0 at MK Dons, leaving Saints in the relegation zone. They were then unbeaten in five games and began a steady climb up the table. An impressive 4-0 win over Exeter on New Year's Day took them into the top two for the first time.

Saints dropped into the playoff places after losing 2-0 at Tranmere Rovers at the end of January, then moved between third and fifth for two months. In April they hit form at the right time, winning nine of their last ten games to finish in second place behind Brighton.

Promotion was effectively secured with a 3-1 win at Plymouth Argyle in the penultimate game. This left Saints three points ahead of Huddersfield Town, with a vastly superior goal difference. They finished the job off on the last day of the season, beating Walsall 3-1 in front of a full house at St Mary's.

FACT 87

2011 RECORD WINNING RUN

Southampton's record run of winning matches is ten. This consisted of victories in the last six games of 2010-11 and the first four of the following season.

The run started on 16th April when Saints beat Bristol Rovers 1-0 at St Mary's. The following week they came from behind to win 2-1 at promotion rivals Brighton, both goals coming in the last six minutes. Two days later on Easter Monday they won 2-0 at home to Hartlepool.

The fourth successive win was a comfortable 3-0 victory over Brentford at Griffin Park. Saints then won 3-1 at Plymouth to leave them on the brink of promotion then confirmed this with a 3-1 home win over Walsall in the final game.

On 6th August, the opening day of 2010-11, Saints beat Leeds 3-1 at St Mary's. They then won 1-0 at Barnsley before an impressive 5-2 victory over Ipswich Town at Portman Road. The tenth straight win was a 1-0 victory over Millwall at St Mary's on 20th August. Both the first and last goals of the run were scored by Guly do Prado.

The run finally came to an end when Saints lost 3-2 at Leicester 27th August. However, by winning the first four games of the season for the first time ever, Saints had provided a springboard for a second successive promotion.

FACT 88
2012
BACK IN
THE PREMIER LEAGUE

Southampton were promoted for the second successive season in 2011-12, taking them back to the Premier League seven years after relegation.

Manager Nigel Adkins didn't make wholesale changes to the Saints squad that had played together in League One. Arguably it was depleted by the sale of Alex Oxlade-Chamberlain to Arsenal for £15 million, but they started off brilliantly, winning their opening four games.

Saints didn't lose momentum and stayed in the top two all season. Rickie Lambert, playing in the second tier for the first time in his career at the age of 29, adapted easily to the higher level and finished as the club's top scorer with 27 league goals. Midfielder Adam Lallana was also undaunted by the step up and got eleven goals from midfield.

The race for automatic promotion went down to the wire, with Saints in a three-way battle alongside Reading and West Ham United. In the penultimate game of the season Saints missed a chance to seal their Premier League place when they lost 2-1 at Middlesbrough.

On 28th April Saints beat Coventry 4-0 at St Mary's to secure second place behind Reading. There were tears of joy at the end of the game as just three years after administration and relegation from the Championship, they were now going back to the Premier League.

2013
TOP SCORER FOR FOURTH SUCCESSIVE SEASON

FACT 89

Rickie Lambert was Southampton's top scorer for the fourth season running in 2012-13, becoming the first player to achieve this since Mick Channon. Lambert's achievement was even more remarkable as he hadn't even played in the Championship prior to the previous season.

When Saints paid £1 million to Bristol Rovers for Lambert following relegation in 2009, they did so in the knowledge he was a proven League One scorer. Lambert ended 2009-10 with 31 league goals, making him the top scorer across England's four divisions. However, Saints failed to make the playoffs due to the points deduction imposed as a result of administration.

In 2010-11 he scored 21 times as Saints secured promotion back to the Championship. 2011-12 was Lambert's thirteenth season in league football, but his first in the second tier. He struck 27 times as Saints were promoted again and was named championship Player of the year.

In his first ever Premier League appearance, Lambert scored for Saints when he came on as a substitute against Manchester City. He featured in all 38 league games, scoring fifteen goals to finish as the club's top scorer again. In August 2013 he made his England debut and at the end of the 2013-14 season made a dream move to Liverpool, the club who had released him as a teenager.

FACT 90
2014 BIGGEST PREMIER LEAGUE WIN

On 14th October 2014 Southampton beat Sunderland 8-0 at St Mary's. It was their biggest ever win in the Premier League, equalling their other record victory since joining the Football League in 1920.

Sunderland defender Santiago Vergini opened the scoring for Saints in the twelfth minute with a spectacular own goal from just inside the area. Close range finishes from Graziano Pellè and Jack Cork then gave Saints a comfortable 3-0 half time lead.

Saints' fourth was also an own goal, this time from Liam Bridcutt, who turned the ball into the net when trying to clear. Pellè then got his second before Dusan Tadic intercepted a poor pass from Sunderland's keeper to score the sixth from thirty yards. Victor Wanyama got the seventh with an unstoppable shot and Sadio Mane completed the rout four minutes from full time.

The 8-0 victory was Saints' biggest in the Premier League and their joint record victory since joining the Football League in 1920. The other 8-0 score line had been back in 1921, when Northampton were beaten in a Third Division South fixture.

FACT 91

2015
THE FASTEST PREMIER LEAGUE HAT TRICK

On 16th May 2015 Southampton's Sadio Mane scored the fastest hat trick in Premier League history. It took the Senegal international striker just two minutes and 56 seconds to score three goals in a 6-1 win over Aston Villa.

Mane's opener came after his first effort had been blocked by keeper Shay Given, but the ball bounced favourably into his path and he turned it into an empty net. His second again had an element of good fortune. A poor back pass saw the ball break loose after Given failed to reach it and Mane was first to react to score from a tight angle.

There was no luck at all attached to the third goal. Shane Long broke down the left and crossed for Mane who scored with a well-placed finish from the edge of the area. Saints were now 3-0 up after just sixteen minutes and eventually won 6-1.

The hat trick, timed at two minutes and 56 seconds, knocked more than a minute and a half off the previous Premier League record set by Liverpool's Robbie Fowler in 1994. Mane hadn't set the record for the fastest hat trick in English football though, which is claimed by Bournemouth's James Hayter in 2004. He scored three against Wrexham in just two minutes twenty seconds.

FACT 92
2016 EUROPA LEAGUE GROUP STAGE EXIT

Southampton had an agonising exit from the group stage of the Europa League in 2016-17. A 1-1 draw between Saints and Israel's Hapoel Be'er Sheva meant both sides finished level on points but the visitors went through as they had a better head to head record.

Saints went straight into the group stages of the Europa League after a sixth place Premier League finish. They began with a convincing 3-0 win over Sparta Prague at St Mary's before drawing 0-0 in Be'er Sheva. They then lost 1-0 away to Inter Milan, before beating the Italian giants 2-1 after being a goal down in a memorable game at St Mary's.

Despite losing 1-0 in Prague, Saints knew that a win or 0-0 draw at home to Be'er Sheva would be enough to progress. With twelve minutes remaining, the visitors took the lead with their first shot on target. Virgil van Dijk equalised in injury time and Saints piled on the pressure, but Maya Yoshida's last gasp header was just wide.

Although Saints had a superior goal difference, the table was decided by head-to-head results if teams had the same number of points. This meant the Israelis progressed on away goals, joining Sparta Prague in the knockout stages.

FACT 93
2017 LEAGUE CUP FINAL HEARTBREAK

Southampton were left heartbroken when they were beaten in the 2017 League Cup final by a late Manchester United goal. Saints had bravely fought back from 2-0 down after having what they thought was the opening goal ruled out for offside.

Manolo Gabbiadini found the net from close range early on, but Ryan Bertrand was adjudged to be offside even though he was out of the action. Zlatan Ibrahimovic then put United ahead with a nineteenth minute free kick and Jesse Lingaard doubled it seven minutes before half time.

Gabbiadini gave Saints hope when scored in first half injury time. Three minutes after the break Saints fans went wild when Gabbiadini equalised, firing home after Steven Davis had headed a corner into his path. Oriol Romeu saw an effort hit the woodwork as Saints remained on top.

With extra time looming and Saints tiring, Ibrahimovic scored three minutes from the end. There was no way back for Saints who were devastated at the end, with United manager Jose Mourinho looking more relieved than elated.

Saints had done themselves proud but that was little consolation given the disallowed goal. Manager Claude Puel said afterwards "Perhaps we deserve better. Manolo Gabbiadini scored three good goals (including the disallowed goal). There's a lot of disappointment of course. We had a fantastic game without the reward."

FACT 94

2018
THE SWANSEA HOTEL DEBACLE

Southampton escaped relegation from the Premier League on the last day of the 2017-18 season. They stayed up at the expense of Swansea, who they beat a few days earlier despite what was dubbed "The Swansea Hotel Debacle."

Saints endured a dreadful run of just one win in 22 games which saw them slide into the relegation zone. Mark Hughes replaced the sacked Mauricio Pelligrino in March and a 2-1 win over Bournemouth on 28th April lifted Saints out of the bottom three. They then drew 1-1 at Everton before a trip to Swansea, who they led on goal difference, for the penultimate game.

Saints were scheduled to stay at the Marriott Hotel in Swansea but their booking was switched to Cardiff at late notice due to a virus outbreak. Dark forces were suspected, but Hughes said it was only a motivating factor for the players.

The match itself was a tense one, with few chances in the first half. After 72 minutes, Saints were awarded a corner from which Manolo Gabbiadini bundled the ball into the net after Charlie Austin's effort was saved. Saints held on for a victory that virtually guaranteed their survival due to their superior goal difference. Three days later their Premier league status was assured despite a late 1-0 home defeat to Manchester City.

FACT 95
2018 SOUTHAMPTON FC WOMEN

In 2018 Southampton FC Women were created, as the club looked to take advantage of the growing interest in the women's game across the country.

This was not the first women's team linked to Saints. In 1970 female fans of the club formed Southampton Women's FC although there was no formal affiliation. They had great success, winning the Women's FA Cup eight times in eleven seasons between 1971 and 1981. The club is still in existence today and was in the same league as Southampton FC Women in 2021.

Between 1995 and 2005 the linked Southampton Saints enjoyed mixed success, yo-yoing between the Southern Premier League and National Premier League, as well as reaching the FA Cup final. When Saints men's team were relegated from the Premier League, support for the women's club was withdrawn. That club eventually folded in 2019.

For Southampton Women's inaugural season in 2018, they were placed in the Southern Region Premier Division after an unsuccessful application to join the Women's Championship. This was the fifth tier and the strong squad that had been assembled enjoyed a perfect season. They won all eighteen games to secure promotion and also beat Oxford City in the final of the League Cup.

FACT 96
2019
FASTEST GOAL IN PREMIER HISTORY

When Southampton played at Watford on 23rd April 2019, Shane Long broke the record for the fastest goal in Premier League history. His effort was timed at just 7.69 seconds.

From the kick-off, the ball was played back to Watford defender Craig Cathcart. His attempted pass was charged down by Long who ran forward and chipped the ball over the advancing keeper.

At 7.69 seconds, Long's goal knocked a clear two seconds off the previous record of 9.82, set by Ledley King for Tottenham Hotspur against Bradford City in 2000.

Despite taking such an early lead, Saints failed to build on it and were undone by a last-minute Watford equaliser by Andre Gray. It meant that Saints were still not totally safe from relegation, having a five-point cushion with three games still to play.

Long's Premier League record is still some way off the record for the fastest goal in any of English football's four divisions. That goes to Jim Fryatt, whose goal for Bradford Park Avenue against Tranmere Rovers in 1964 was timed at exactly four seconds on the referee's stopwatch.

FACT 97
2019
BIGGEST WIN
AT FRATTON PARK

Southampton won 4-0 at Portsmouth in the third round of the League Cup on 24th September 2019. It was their first win at Fratton Park since 1984 and their biggest overall.

It was the first meeting of the two clubs for seven years. It may have been 'only the League Cup' but neither side wanted to lose this match. Saints had a strong line-up but it was Portsmouth who had the best of the early chances, hitting the post and having a shot cleared off the line.

After 21 minutes Danny Ings eased Saints fans' nerves when his low shot from outside the area found the net. A minute from half time Ings doubled the lead, latching on to a through ball by Michael Obafemi to score.

In the second half Saints easily kept Portsmouth at bay, limiting them to long range efforts. Their Premier League status then shone through as they scored two more towards the end of the game. Cédric Soares scored the third in the 77th minute and four minutes from time Nathan Redmond's strike made it 4-0.

The score line surpassed Saints' previous biggest win at Fratton Park, a 5-2 league victory in 1966. It was also their first victory there since a 1-0 win in an FA Cup tie in 1984.

FACT 98
2019
RECORD DEFEAT

On 25th October 2019 Southampton were thrashed 9-0 at St Mary's by Leicester City. It was the club's record defeat and also the biggest ever away win in English topflight history.

Saints fell behind in the tenth minute to a goal by Ben Chilwell. VAR then intervened and ordered the sending off, of Saints' defender Ryan Bertrand for a two footed challenge during the build-up that had gone unnoticed by the referee. Saints capitulated and were 5-0 down at half time.

Manager Ralph Hasenhüttl made two changes during the break as he aimed for damage limitation, replacing centre forward Danny Ings with an extra defender. However, within fifteen minutes of the restart Saints were 7-0 down. For 25 minutes there were no more goals. The eighth came with four minutes remaining and then deep into injury time Jamie Vardy's penalty made it 9-0.

The ninth goal meant it was Saints worst ever defeat and also created a topflight record for an away win, stretching back to 1888. The players and coaches later donated wages to the Saints Foundation charity. The record defeat was then equalled in 2021, when Saints lost 9-0 at Manchester United in another game where they suffered an early sending off.

FACT 99
2020
BEHIND CLOSED DOORS AND WAGE DEFERRALS

The Covid-19 pandemic meant that Southampton, along with the rest of the Premier League, completed the 2019-20 season behind closed doors. The players were also the first from any Premier League club to agree to wage deferrals to protect other staff.

On 7th March 2020 Saints lost 1-0 at home to Newcastle, a result that left them fourteenth in the table. Eleven days later the Premier League was suspended due to the Covid-19 pandemic.

On 9th April the club confirmed that manager Ralph Hasenhüttl, his coaching staff and the first team squad had agreed to defer part of their salaries for that month, as well as May and June. Press reports quoted the figures as between 10% and 30%.

A club statement said it was "to help protect the future of the club, the staff that work within it and the community we serve." The decision came at a time when senior politicians were criticising clubs for using the government job retention scheme to pay salaries. Saints confirmed they would be covering all costs themselves.

When the Premier League resumed at the end of June, it was with all games played in empty stadiums. Saints lost only one in their last nine matches, finishing eleventh in the table.

FACT 100

2021
FIRST FANS AT WEMBLEY

After more than a year of matches being played behind closed doors at Wembley, Southampton fans were among the first allowed back on 18th April 2021. However, numbers were extremely limited and those that did attend were disappointed as Saints lost the FA Cup semi-final to Leicester City.

Restrictions due to the Covid-19 pandemic went on far longer than anybody could have initially envisaged. All games at England's national stadium for a whole calendar year from late March 2020 were played behind closed doors.

Saints reached the semi-finals of the FA Cup by beating Shrewsbury, Arsenal, Wolverhampton and Bournemouth. All of these games were played in empty stadiums. The government announced that their semi-final would be one of several test events aimed at getting spectators safely back into sports stadiums.

There were serious restrictions on the ticket allocation, as only residents from the Wembley area were allowed to apply for the maximum of 4,000 available. Those attending also had to show proof of a negative Covid test and wear face masks at their seats.

Sadly for Saints they failed to rise to the occasion. They didn't have a single shot on goal in the first half and although they did better after the break, Kelechi Iheanacho's 55th minute goal was enough to take Leicester to the final.

The 100 Facts Series

Arsenal, *Steve Horton*	978-1-908724-09-0
Aston Villa, *Steve Horton*	978-1-908724-98-4
Brighton, *Steve Horton*	978-1-912782-78-9
Celtic, *Steve Horton*	978-1-908724-10-6
Chelsea, *Kristian Downer*	978-1-908724-11-3
Everton, *Bob Sharp*	978-1-908724-12-0
Hearts, *Steve Horton*	978-1-912782-48-2
Leeds, *Steve Horton*	978-1-908724-94-6
Leicester City, *Steve Horton*	978-1-912782-47-5
Liverpool, *Steve Horton*	978-1-908724-13-7
Manchester City, *Steve Horton*	978-1-908724-14-4
Manchester United, *Iain McCartney*	978-1-908724-15-1
Newcastle United, *Steve Horton*	978-1-908724-16-8
Norwich City, *Steve Horton*	978-1-908724-99-1
Nottingham Forest, *Steve Horton*	978-1-912782-46-8
Rangers, *David Clayton*	978-1-908724-17-5
Sheffield United, *Steve Horton*	978-1-912782-45-1
Southampton, *Steve Horton*	978-1-912782-79-6
Sunderland, *Steve Horton*	978-1-912782-80-2
Tottenham Hotspur, *Steve Horton*	978-1-908724-18-2
West Ham, *Steve Horton*	978-1-908724-80-9

Player Autographs

Player Autographs

Player Autographs